THE EDUCATOR'S GUIDE
TO ALTERNATIVE JOBS & CAREERS

Other books by Ronald L. Krannich

The Almanac of American Government Jobs and Careers
The Almanac of International Jobs and Careers
Careering and Re-Careering For the 1990s
The Complete Guide to International Jobs and Careers
The Complete Guide to Public Employment
Discover the Right Job For You!
Dynamite Cover Letters
Dynamite Resumes
Find a Federal Job Fast!
High Impact Resumes and Letters
Interview For Success
Mayors and Managers
Moving Out of Education
Moving Out of Government
Network Your Way to Job and Career Success
The Politics of Family Planning Policy
Re-Careering in Turbulent Times
Salary Success
Shopping in Exciting Australia and Papua New Guinea
Shopping in Exotic Places
Shopping the Exotic Pacific
Shopping and Traveling in Exotic Asia
Shopping and Traveling in Exotic Hong Kong
Shopping and Traveling in Exotic Indonesia
Shopping and Traveling in Exotic Singapore and Malaysia
Shopping and Traveling in Exotic Thailand
Shopping and Traveling in the Exotic Philippines

THE EDUCATOR'S GUIDE TO ALTERNATIVE JOBS & CAREERS

Ronald L. Krannich, Ph.D.

IMPACT PUBLICATIONS
Woodbridge, VA

THE EDUCATOR'S GUIDE TO ALTERNATIVE JOBS AND CAREERS

Library of Congress Cataloging-in-Publication Data
Krannich, Ronald L.
   The educator's guide to alternative jobs and careers /
   Ronald L. Krannich
      p. cm.
   Includes bibliographical references (p.) and index
   ISBN 0-942710-47-9: $24.95.—ISBN 0-942710-41-X (pbk.):$13.95
   1. Career changes. 2. Job hunting. 3. Occupational mobility
I. Title. II. Title: Educator's guide to alternative jobs and careers
HF5384.K69   1991
650.14'02437—dc20   90-25027
                                                         CIP

Cover designed by ABS Graphics, 8564 Custer Court, Manassas, VA 22111, Tel. 703/361-7415

For information on distribution or quantity discount rates, call (703/361-7300), FAX (703/335-9486), or write to: Sales Department, IMPACT PUBLICATIONS, 4580 Sunshine Court, Woodbridge, VA 22192. Distributed to the trade by National Book Network, 4720 Boston Way, Suite A, Lanham, MD 20706, Tel. 301/459-8696

CONTENTS

PREFACE

Education is a noble, enlightening, and rewarding profession for millions of classroom teachers, researchers, and administrators. However, it also is a limiting career for many individuals who want to achieve more in life than the daily routines of being a teacher, researcher, or administrator. After only a few years of experience, many educators' careers plateau. Furthermore, many feel frustrated with their careers due to a combination of limited career advancement and mobility opportunities, disappointing salary increments, increasing workloads, burdensome bureaucracy, and petty politics. What was ostensibly a noble, enlightening and rewarding profession looks more like many other jobs in society.

The business of education today looks no brighter for educators than the retrenchment years of the 1980s. Numerous educational institutions in the 1990s again will most likely feel the double-whammy of declining enrollments and restrictive budgets due to a combination of changing demographics and hard economic times impacting on the financing of education at all levels.

This book is designed to assist educators in making important career decisions for the 1990s. First published a decade ago in collaboration with William J. Banis as *Moving Out of Education,* this new book builds on the foundation we established in this earlier work. It provides a career and job search roadmap for educators interested in leaving education for other worlds of work. As such, it dispels numerous myths often preventing educators from making career changes and addresses the fears and uncertainties involved in the career change process. Most important of all, it outlines a practical plan of action involving key steps in the career exploration and job search processes: self-assessment, resume and letter writing, researching alternative jobs and careers, networking for informational interviews, interviewing for jobs, and negotiating salaries. Once you complete the following chapters, you should be well on your way to making a positive career change, if that is indeed what you want to do. On the other hand, you may decide to remain in education since such a career best satisfies your goals. Whether you decide to remain in or leave education, this book will help you make the necessary choices.

This is a different book for educators and career planners. It is not a listing of alternative job titles and descriptions that might be interesting to educators. While the book includes such information, it primarily focuses on the *key processes* that will help you find the right job for you. Focusing on the process of self-discovery, it outlines the nuts-and-bolts of putting together a realistic plan of action and then implementing it over a three to six month period.

I wish to thank many educators and career counselors who contributed both directly and indirectly to this book. I especially owe a debt of gratitude to William J. Banis who collaborated with me on two previous books—***Moving Out of Education*** and ***High Impact Resumes and Letters.*** Much of his work and philosophy regarding self-assessment, resumes, and interviews is well represented here. I also owe a special debt of gratitude to my partner, Caryl Rae Krannich. When I refer to *"we"* in the text, I refer to the two of us. She encouraged me to complete this book, spent numerous hours editing it, made valuable suggestions for changes, and contributed to the chapter on interview skills.

As former educators with nearly 40 years of combined experience teaching in secondary schools and universities, we've made our own transition from education. Like many ex-educators, our transition was initially filled with doubts, uncertainties, and false starts. Now with nearly 10 years of hindsight, we know we made the right decision to leave education in the early 1980s. We've discovered what many other ex-educators learn several years after leaving education: there is life after education, and it is much more rewarding than one might expect. You can indeed shape your own future if you are sufficiently motivated and determined to achieve new career goals. But you first need to explore your alternatives and then develop a practical plan of action that will take you where you want to go.

Planning, hard work, determination, and tenacity—valuable skills both developed and reinforced in education—will serve you well as you make your journey beyond education. The pages that follow build on these skills. If you follow them carefully, you will be well on your way to making positive career choices for the 1990s.

Ronald L. Krannich

Chapter One

CAREERS AND EDUCATORS

So you're thinking about leaving education and embarking on a new career where students, administrators, classrooms, committees, bureaucracy, and lengthy vacation periods are but faded memories? Education has been good for you until now, but it may be time to move on to something else for the next 10 to 20 years of your life. ·

What else can you do other than be an educator? What kind of life is there after education? You love teaching, but are there other things you might love doing just as much, if not more? Can you make a career change to something that will be even more rewarding than what you have been doing in education? Let's take a hard look at some uncharted career waters that may well prove to be the best time of your life.

LIFE AFTER EDUCATION

Yes, there is life after education and a wonderful life for those who know the secrets of making positive career transitions from education to other worlds of work. And it's a good idea that you now begin assessing your career future during the next 10 to 20 years. Do you, for example, want to continue teaching the same subjects or further advance up a limited education bureaucratic hierarchy during the next 10 to 20 years, or are you ready to explore some exciting job and career alternatives, many of which you never knew existed?

Many feel they should have made the move earlier—if only they knew then what they know now!

As many ex-educators testify daily, they have discovered rewarding careers outside education that readily use the many skills they acquired in education. Their transition may have been difficult at first—full of doubts, false starts, uncertainty, and failed expectations—but in the long run, leaving education was the right thing to do. In fact, many feel they should have made the move earlier—if only they knew then what they know now!

Like any job or career, education has its share of positives and negatives. For some people, it's a wonderful career which they entered just out of college and continued until retirement at age 65. For others, it was an interesting career for the first 5 to 10 years, but for them leaves much to be desired over the next 10 to 20 years, especially since their interests and goals have changed during this time.

TAKE CHARGE OF YOUR FUTURE

But what can *you* do outside education, and how can *you* best make a career transition a reality in today's job market? The following pages provide practical answers to these key questions.

This book is not about the problems of education and why you should leave. Many of the problems and frustrations are legend—low salaries, plateaued careers, limited advancement opportunities, bureaucracy and red tape, low student achievement, depressing educational environments, petty politics, stress, and high competition for low stakes. While many of these problems are unique to education and teaching, many also are found in other types of jobs. They may or may not affect you depending on your situation.

More often than not, however, we hear from educators who sum up their problems as follows:

"I've had it. It's time I did something else with my life."

These are not people who casually wonder about life after education and thus wish to *"test the waters"* to see if the grass is greener on the other side—just in case they find something interesting. Rather, these are highly motivated individuals who are ready to do something positive about their future. This statement probably summarizes the culmination of many career frustrations—unhappy relationships with students, administrators, and colleagues; disappointing salary increments, benefits, promotions, and recognition; increasing workloads involving activities unrelated to their interests and skills; and new goals that cannot be fulfilled in education. In other words, their career in education has plateaued at a frustrating level where the future looks increasingly routine, stressful, and hopeless. Reality is no longer in line with expectations.

Nor is this book a listing of alternative job titles educators might find interesting. Several books already do this with questionable relevance for their readers. This book does much more than this. It's all about taking charge of your future by examining:

- Where you are at present (assessment)
- What you do well (abilities and skills)
- What you enjoy doing (interests and values)
- Where you want to go (goals and objectives)
- How to get there (strategies for success)

As such, this book is designed to help you create your own blueprint for career success outside education in the decade ahead. If you follow it carefully, it will help you decide where you want to go and then show you how to get there.

Let's be perfectly clear what we are doing and where we are going. We don't tell educators what they should do. After all, individual needs and situations differ. We outline in detail many of the most advanced methods for making the transition from education to other rewarding jobs and careers.

This may be a disturbing book for many educators who are fervently committed to their profession; who call for professional renewal rather than abandonment to resolve the problems of education; and who disdain status, money, and material pleasure for more altruistic pursuits within their profession. Education needs such people; we admire their dedication and spirit and wish them well. On the other hand, we address the concerns of many educators who believe they and their families deserve better.

This is a very different book for educators. We outline how they can move into more rewarding and satisfying careers that are compatible with their interests, skills, and goals. Above all, we attempt to take the fear and frustration out of thinking and doing the unknown—leaving education. If you have been in education all your life, you should find this book both challenging and exhilarating.

Our methods require you to first clarify your thinking about yourself and your future and then develop a realistic plan of action. For to leave education without a clear idea of who you are and where you want to go can lead to new disappointments and frustrated career moves.

THE BUSINESS OF EDUCATION

For many educators, the business of education has little to do with education. Instead, economics, politics, and bureaucracy often dominate the jobs of educators. Teachers increasingly find themselves working on peripheral concerns of education. Given the present structure and environment of education, it's a wonder education does as well as it does.

Indeed, education is a fickled business. Its continuing growth is dependent upon a combination of favorable demographics and economic conditions. The past decade, however, has witnessed unfavorable demographics as well as a boom/bust economy that will continue to have negative implications for the careers of educators in the coming decade.

Once a growing, dynamic, and promising industry, education and the education profession are again treading troubled waters in the 1990s. Declining enrollments, boom/bust economic cycles, restrictive budgets, contentious colleagues, and new legal and bureaucratic requirements have created several negative scenarios for educators. As the post-World War II baby boom generation completed its education in the 1960s and 1970s, elementary and secondary teachers found fewer students to teach. In many communities—especially in the large urban centers of the northeast and north central regions—declining student enrollments during the 1970s and 1980s resulted in a decade of serious retrenchment—from closing schools and firing teachers to limiting salary increments and promotions. Demand for teachers has been largely restricted to a few communities experiencing major population growth (southeast, southwest, and northwest) and to a few subject areas where teacher shortages are most pronounced (math and science).

The downturns in elementary and secondary education were also felt in higher education during the 1980s. The great expansion of programs, faculty, and facilities of the 1960s and 1970s was all but over by 1980. Except for a few elite private, well endowed institutions that continued to grow, many public institutions of higher education retrenched with leaner budgets as fewer traditional students entered their doors. Programs and faculty in education, the social sciences, and the humanities—lacking a ready market of future elementary and secondary teachers to train as well as fewer students choosing such fields of study—were hit the hardest. In many institutions, scarce resources were reallocated to growing programs that showed greater perceived job relevance for students—business, computer science, and allied health professions.

Difficult years continue to lie ahead for institutions, faculty, staff, and administrators who remain in education.

While individual scenarios may differ, the overall prognosis is the same: difficult years continue to lie ahead for institutions, faculty, staff, and administrators who remain in education. Continuing demographic downturns, economic stagnation, and government budgetary crises translate into fewer students, constrained resources, limited salary increases, and fewer promotions and perks in education at all levels. Regardless of public rhetoric about the 1990s being the *"decade of education"*, the 1990s will most likely be a decade of financial crisis for education. The key question is who will pay the costly bills to maintain the present system of education.

The coming crisis is readily predictable, and it has negative implications for careers of educators. The demographics for the 1990s, for example, continue to look unfavorable for education. Since Americans are having fewer children, in the next two decades fewer students will attend the schools that were built and staffed for the baby boom generation of more than a decade ago. The boom/bust economy of the 1980s will likely be repeated throughout the 1990s. Indeed, the bust cycle began again in 1990 as another recession seriously affected state and local tax bases that largely fuel elementary, secondary, and higher education. Unlike the recession of the early 1980s, this one will likely have more serious long-term implications for financing public education: education will feel the triple-whammy of (1) a declining property tax base, due to the depressed private housing market; (2) widespread anti-tax sentiment that will prevent significant increases in other taxes to offset the losses in revenue normally programmed for education; and (3) changing demographics of fewer school-age children and young adults. Accordingly, many educators must choose between two career futures: stay in education to compete for scarcer resources in retrenching institutions or leave education to advance their careers.

Business again looks stagnant these days in education. Regardless of creative efforts to ward off the worst effects of retrenchment, the business of education is not likely to get better during the next decade. As in the early 1980s, educators will again need to lower their expectations and live with less status and financial security. Many have done so already. For example, elementary and secondary schools discourage new teachers with low wages. Higher education institutions encourage transient faculty and low morale by hiring more part-time faculty, awarding tenure to fewer faculty members, and paying low beginning salaries. Older experienced teachers receive disincentives such as increased workloads, inadequate wages, and threats of job loss. Many teachers cannot support a family on an educator's salary—or even two educator's salaries—nor can they find adequate opportunities to supplement their incomes. These educators need to face the truth about going nowhere as well as learn how to avoid an even more stagnating future in education.

Moving up within education by getting an M.A. or Ph.D. degree to teach in junior colleges, colleges, or universities is a sure way to further depress one's career. As with elementary and secondary education, faculty and administrators in colleges and universities are experiencing their own difficult times.

What happens to educators in such situations? For elementary and secondary education, one frequent outcome is tensions and conflicts among school board members, parents, teachers, and administrators. Young teachers are terminated in order to keep tenured, and sometimes less able, teachers. Superintendents become immersed in crisis management, and many get fired. Contentious relationships and petty politics among faculty and administrators dominate what is education's classic career scenario:

high competition for low stakes. So much energy gets expended on fighting over trivia. Overall, many people are unnecessarily hurt in such situations. Others survive with a few scars. Hardly anyone gets by without some damage.

Contentious relationships and petty politics among faculty and administrators dominate what is education's classic career scenario: high competition for low stakes.

There's a time in everyone's life when they need to step back and assess their job and career. Expanding their thinking by looking outside their current work environment, they need to see the larger picture of jobs and careers best suited for their interests, abilities, and goals. Above all, they need to re-examine their goals—many of which may have changed during the past few years. Ideally, this assessment should be done every year as part of an *"annual career checkup"*. However, most people only do this when their careers are in trouble or when they become highly motivated to think the unthinkable—possibly moving out of education and into a more rewarding career.

Let's look at two scenarios in higher education from the perspectives of individual faculty members. If you change the cast of characters and the institutional settings, these scenarios are similarly pertinent to elementary and secondary education. If you think you can improve your career by moving into higher education, you should take a hard look at several realities relating to retrenchment.

JUST STARTING OUT

You receive your M.A. or Ph.D. You're proud of your achievement and excited about your future as an academician. You think you're going somewhere. Now, on to your first job. You hope it's with a good university, maybe not as good as the one you graduated from, but good nonetheless. You want to teach bright students; publish in major scholarly journals; go to conferences and present thought-provoking papers before your peers; make an impact on your profession; get tenured and promoted to full professor; take long vacations and enjoy a secure and leisurely lifestyle; work with interesting and talented people; and thoroughly enjoy your work. You are joining the ranks of a noble profession of respectable individuals who seek to advance knowledge and discover truth. Status and promotion rewards go to those who work hard, are dedicated, and produce quality work. You're lucky to have such a job. You are convinced a cruel world of politics, deception, dishonesty, and greed exists in jobs and careers outside education.

But as you make the transition from graduate student to faculty colleague, new experiences in the day-to-day business of education have a way of disturbing your idealism and optimism. You begin your first teaching job at an undistinguished but pretentious medium-sized university located in a small town that boasts a Kmart, McDonald's, Taco Bell, and a condominium. You start at $24,000 a year—it's better than the $6,000 a year you made as someone's assistant in graduate school and, after all, money really isn't that important in the larger scheme of things. The faculty and administration claim this institution is really going places—we'll be in the big league in no time—and they need people with your credentials to help build the institution. So you're important to their future—that's flattering. You take the job with the expectation of eventually moving on to a really good university, once you've made your mark here. You need to start somewhere. This is the best offer you have in today's job market; indeed, you're lucky you even got *this* job!

With a heavy workload of teaching four or five courses a semester, plus advising and committee work, you feel you are a jack-of-all-trades. They want you to teach everything in sight, regardless of your training and interests. You work 70-hour weeks as a dedicated teacher, researcher, community servant, and emerging scholar in your field. You're good at what you do, even though you are doing too much. You rationalize your workload by convincing yourself that this is an important first stepping stone to better things to come in your profession.

But after three years, unexpectedly you are told that you will no longer be retained, because you don't measure up to the high standards of your mediocre department, school, or university—although no one knows exactly what those standards are. You sense something went wrong, terribly wrong, but you're not sure what it was. You now know this isn't what you expected when you were in graduate school planning your bright future in academia.

You know you deserved better. You are one of the most productive and competent faculty members at this institution. In fact, you are a rate-breaker who makes others envious of your professional accomplishments. Your superiors—individuals of limited achievement outside this institution—do a great deal of university politicking; they curry favor with their superiors; they attempt to impress their subordinates with the number and quality of committee assignments and social invitations they receive; and they talk a lot about what a great university they're building. Too bad you won't be around for the self-congratulatory speeches that come at the beginning and end of the academic year. These people are politically entrenched with tenure, seniority, perks, and the right set of survival and promotional relationships. You have been dealt with unjustly and unprofessionally, but your only way up in the academic career game is to get out of your present institution without making too big of a fuss; the people may be vindictive if you fight them. Lawyers cost more money than your job is worth. You're a realist, so you go job-hunting—most likely for a similar position at another academic institution—where this scenario may or may not be repeated again. Maybe this was just an unlucky first job. Or perhaps your problem is not unique? You begin hearing more and more stories, with similar themes, from friends and colleagues at other academic institutions. Can this be true elsewhere? Is there something about the structure of higher education that generates this type of career environment?

Sound familiar? If not, let's try a second scenario which may be more relevant to your situation.

STAYED AROUND TOO LONG

This time you receive tenure and are promoted to associate professor. However, you soon discover this long sought-after security has unanticipated costs. Younger academicians, just out of graduate school and with low salary expectations, are eager for work. Since the administration prefers hiring such Ph.D.s, if it weren't for the security of tenure, you would probably lose your present job to one of them.

You have mellowed with age. Your research and publication productivity has declined. You are less marketable today as a secure tenured associate professor than when you were an insecure nontenured assistant professor. Teaching and administrative duties are now routine; they lack the challenge and excitement they had when they were new and unfamiliar. The real value of your salary continues to decline in the face of increasing inflation and meager salary increments. Your 25-year old former students, who graduated with bachelor's degrees four years ago, are now making $15,000 a year more than you—and they will more than double your salary in another four years. While you would like to send your two children to an outstanding college, you can't afford $17,000 per child on your $34,000 annual salary. Maybe you could move into university administration? But few if any opportunities are available for you, since other faculty members are eager to do the same. Besides, you're not sure you would like the lifestyle of an administrator. Best to stay where you are and, in the meantime, maybe things will improve at the university. Maybe the budget will increase; maybe a new president or dean will be hired; or maybe you'll get a nice research grant that will enable you to do some other things and receive additional compensation?

But let's face it, nothing's really getting better. Enrollments are declining, the budget must be cut by 10 percent, and the university administration is talking again about re-examining the tenure policy; actually they need to make internal personal *"adjustments"* in light of new economic realities facing the institution. However, 75 percent of the budget already goes to personnel, and pruning the budget usually means cutting personnel. This time it means terminating both tenured and nontenured faculty. Faculty morale declines accordingly; the once collegial atmosphere of trust and mutual respect leads to distrust, suspicion, envy, and vindictiveness as petty politics take center stage in the drama of retrenchment. Changes in administrative personnel—dean, vice-president, and president—are supposed to result in more productivity. However, *"productivity"* is really a euphemism for *"retrenchment"*. This is not what they taught you in graduate school when you were committing yourself to this career!

The name of the game is *"survival"* and *"holding your own ground"*. Retrenchment politics become somewhat ruthless and unprofessional. You sense the new administrators are rearranging the deck chairs on the Titanic. Within three to five years they will probably move on to other institutions where they will convince another governing board that they can save another sinking ship by being hard-nosed about financial and personnel matters. They talk about quality, but they are experts at cutting budgets and firing faculty. They—along with their well groomed administrative entourages and consultant-friends—constitute a new breed of pragmatic administrators in higher education. They are the middlemen supposedly saving educational institutions from the axes of politicians and from the unrealistic demands of discontented, self-centered faculty members.

You discover you're trapped with tenure. The security is nice, but you really want out. However, you don't know what to do or where to go. At times you have second thoughts, because your low paying job looks relatively good in the face of a tight job market and compared to the plight of nontenured faculty members these days. Worst of all, tenure may not be as secure as you thought since more and more tenured faculty are being terminated.

You are lucky to have tenure. But are you? Compared to whom and what? Your options have been limited by tenure. You have security—for now—but this security has psychological and material costs. Contrary to what many people think, you are not deadwood. You feel underemployed, over-worked with trivia, and unappreciated and neglected by your superiors and colleagues. You look forward to those long vacations that you were told were the rewards of academia—even though you work without compensation during most vacations. You often think of retiring at age 65. Retirement comes with a complimentary university rocking chair; hand shakes and pats on the back from administrators and fellow faculty members for your *"great contributions"* ; testimonials from your more appreciative former students; a small pension; and lifetime access to the university library, faculty dining room, and perhaps your department's copy machine. You take pride in the fact that so many of your students became successful in their careers—moreso than you—and you take some of the credit for their successes—justifiably or not. You occasionally wonder how different life would have been had you not received tenure. What ever happened to your former colleagues who were denied tenure?

LIVING IN THE REAL WORLD

These and other comparable scenarios are found throughout higher, secondary, and elementary education. This is not to say that all educators are unhappy or suffer from a bad case of *"false consciousness"*. Many are happy, satisfied, and productive and wouldn't trade their present positions for anything or any money. They thrive in educational environments; some work in growing institutions. A few others are even financially well off due to a combination of early promotions, seniority, book royalties, and consulting activities.

We believe the happy, enthusiastic, and prosperous educators are becoming fewer in number. Many colleges and universities continue to show signs of retrenching institutions which seek survival by inflating grades, lowering admissions standards, reducing the percentage of tenured faculty, increasing the number of part-time teachers, abolishing programs, and intensely lobbying state legislators and the federal government. Similar to the 1980s, the double-whammy for educational institutions during the 1990s is declining enrollments and rising costs. The triple-whammy for faculty members is heavier workloads, decreased job security, and higher costs of living attendant with inflation and low salary increments.

The effects of retrenchment on institutions and individuals was evident during the 1980s and will most likely continue during the 1990s. Programs and departments were eliminated in many colleges and universities. Several small colleges closed and many others are likely to do so in the near future. Nearly everywhere faculty lost influence in university governance; greater erosion of faculty influence is likely to continue over the coming decade.

Many educators are returning to the "good ole days" when teachers constituted an economically marginal class in society.

Personnel problems and debilitating internal politics have occurred in many retrenching institutions. Indeed, university presidents admit that next to financial problems, personnel problems are their biggest headache. Such an environment breeds the very evils that academicians have long associated with the *"cruelness"* of the nonacademic world. During the 1980s, many colleges and universities appeared under siege with internal personnel and political problems associated with retrenchment. Academic vindictiveness and intolerance—ostensibly relating to questions of individual merit and productivity but actually centering on issues of personalities and lifestyles—were increasingly aired in public. Survival was *"in"* and quality and excellence was *"out"* as the American Association of University Professors (AAUP) reported an overflow of *"mean little cases"* centering on controversial tenure, promotion, and salary decisions.

While such behavior is known to occur outside academe, it has been increasingly aired in public as faculty members have become more litigious in dealing with issues of equity and fairness. Stripped of the idealism, mythology, and mysticism that insulates education from the *"other"* world, educators, too, have *"dirty laundry"* in their closets. Academicians, like normal people, go through job stress and mid-career crises; many have ulcers and problems with nerves; and some work with superiors and colleagues who are entrenched incompetents. Many educators are treated unfairly, but like most poor people, they lack the power to do something about it. Many educators are returning to the *"good ole days"* when teachers constituted an economically marginal class in society. Educators also are involved in all kinds of internal politics that inequitably distribute the decreasing rewards their institutions have to offer. In fact, academic politics may be more complex and debilitating than politics in other organizations.

THE CAREER DISTURBED

An increasing number of educators are becoming career disturbed and anxious about their futures. Career disturbed educators have one or more of the following characteristics:

- Being terminated for every conceivable reason, from budgetary cuts to insubordination and incompetence.

- Increasingly aware of receiving disincentives such as low salary increments and heavier workloads.

- Dissatisfied with their jobs due to disincentives, interpersonal problems, dull work, and failed expectations.

- Established achievement and monetary goals which cannot be met within education.

- Want more challenging and rewarding careers but don't know how to make the transition from education to other occupations.

- Enjoy their work but can't make ends meet if they continue in education.

While many educators want out, they are caught in the academic trap of being over-specialized in particular disciplines, uncertain what they can do besides teaching and research, or are afraid to abandon the seeming security of tenure.

Since the early 1980s many professional associations and universities responded to the career needs of educators by offering workshops, seminars, and special programs focusing on alternative careers for educators. Most efforts have been aimed at showing educators how to make a career transition from academe to business, industry, and government. Six-week programs, such as the Career Opportunities Institute at the University of Virginia, taught participants how to organize a career development plan, conduct career research for identifying career alternatives, write resumes and letters, develop job contacts, and conduct job interviews as well as introduced them to the basic principles, issues, and questions of business administration.

GOING ELSEWHERE BY DESIGN

Thousands of career disturbed and anxious educators need practical career assistance for the 1990s. Many elementary and secondary teachers are becoming more anxious as they fail to advance within education by acquiring more graduate degrees. Many tenured and nontenured faculty members, who already moved into higher education, are seeking a way out of their present jobs. Many university administrators, who formerly held academic positions, also are looking for a way out of education. Many graduate students contemplating academic careers seek information on the job market as well as job search techniques. And many educators approaching retirement age want to explore new careers beyond education. The purpose of this book is to help these people guide their careers into the most productive channels possible.

This is a no-nonsense *"how-to"* book written specifically for educators. It is designed to be simple and jargon-free. However, educators normally do not read this type of material, because they are suspicious of simplistic *"yes/no"* or *"how-to"* answers to complex questions, and because they prefer aesthetic, descriptive, explanatory, and theory-building literature in the specialized languages of their disciplines. However, we see no alternative way to address this problem. Other *"how-to"* career planning literature is not designed to deal with the unique career problems of educators. Therefore, our approach is both applied and prescriptive; it is a mixture of empirical research, experience, intuition, common sense, and faith. We explain the problem of educational careers and outline proven methods for identifying and finding rewarding careers outside education.

This is a nuts-and-bolts book about a problem and how to solve it. It provides no magical formulas nor demands skills other than those you already possess and enjoy using. Many of the methods are validated in the social science research findings of psychologists, sociologists, economists, and political scientists. Individuals in these disciplines will find that this book transforms several of their explanatory theories—especially role and social network—into prescriptions for conducting an effective job search.

Educators who begin and remain in a single educational position throughout their worklife are anomalies in today's dynamic job market.

Let's start with some basic facts and assumptions about the nature of careers and the educational marketplace and outline a few rules for getting you started on your job search. First, most individuals entering the workplace now experience many career and job changes throughout their lives. Since jobs and careers are dynamic, changing, and unpredictable, you should view your present job and career as temporary. Educators who begin and remain in a single educational position throughout their worklife are anomalies in today's dynamic job market.

Second, you should be prepared to change jobs and careers with the minimum amount of psychological and financial trauma. A job change—voluntary or forced—should result in healthy career advancement. Since a career consists of a series of related jobs, the best way to advance your career is to plan for job changes. Unfortunately, most people become victims of the job market. For example, it is a national tragedy to find highly skilled Ph.D.s, who have a great deal of time and money invested in their educations, performing jobs ill-suited to their interests, abilities, and skills. There is no reason—other than short-sightedness—for these people to be driving trucks, pumping gas, or waiting on tables, unless they really desire such career alternatives. Above all, you should take charge of your future by finding jobs and careers that are **right for you.** The pages that follow will show you how to do this.

Third, many people are unhappy as well as underemployed in their present jobs. When was the last early Monday morning you couldn't wait to get to the office to begin working? When was the last Friday afternoon you became depressed, because you had to leave your job? If you can't answer these questions with recent dates, chances are you belong to the ranks of the unhappy workers who experience the *"Monday morning blues"*—knowing they have five more days to go—and the *"Thank God it's Friday joys"*—two days before the *"Monday morning blues"* begin again. Some estimate that the leading cause of health problems in this country is job unhappiness, stress, and depression. If you belong to this group, you should seriously consider learning all you can about how to get out of your present job and into one that is more satisfying. We urge you to start right now; set a firm date when you will start your new career. Keep this date in mind as you consider the advice in the following pages for developing and implementing your own career plan.

Fourth, assuming you belong to a troubled industry, it may be best that you get out rather than stay in. Numerous educational institutions provide ample evidence that people who stay around get hurt unnecessarily. You should not become another victim of such an institution. Analyze your situation; consider getting out before it's too late and before the damage is too extensive. There are immediate advantages to getting out. You will improve your chances of realizing your potential as well as achieving both personal and professional success. Ironically, you may actually improve education by releasing some of the personnel pressure that is so central to its present problems.

Fifth, since you are well educated, it is assumed you can learn on your own when information is presented in a clear, concise, and self-directed format. For the cover price of this book, you should be able to do most of what you would learn through an expensive workshop, institute, seminar, or consulting organization. The costs of these structured learning experiences range anywhere from $100 for a workshop to $5,000 or more for the services of a professional organization. However, depending on your needs, you may want to use some of these services. This book will help you evaluate which are best for you.

Sixth in order to benefit directly from this book, you must put it into practice. We know, based on others' experiences in writing *"how-to"* books and from clients, that only a small percentage of individuals who seek career assistance ever follow through in implementing it. As you put into practice the many principles and strategies outlined in this book, consider several prerequisites for making them work for you:

1. **You must develop a positive mental attitude** about yourself and your capacity to succeed in finding a job that is right for you. If you are negative or pessimistic, you will program yourself for failure. Your attitude will make a big difference in how well you make these strategies work for you.

2. **You must continuously ask questions about jobs and careers.** You will learn the most from others. Keep thinking about job alternatives. Talk to successful and positive people. People generally like to be helpful and give advice. However, some of the worst people to consult may be fellow educators; you may threaten their sense of security and create conflict for them by considering leaving education.

3. **You must set goals and plan accordingly.** Your goals should be periodically reassessed in light of new information, knowledge, and interests. This is a learning experience, and thus you should be open to new information and willing to change your thinking if necessary. Without goals you will be going nowhere. Plan your job search and work your plan.

4. **You must be committed to working hard at finding a job.** Finding a good job may be the hardest work you ever do. A successful job search requires time, commitment, and persistent effort. Devote time each day to your job search. We know of no shortcuts in this process.

5. **You must like to meet and work with people.** Job hunting is a social process. If you lack initiative or are an academic recluse, this book will disappoint you. If you are shy, our approaches will help you; they are neither *"pushy"* nor *"aggressive"* for making new contacts. Overall, our approaches should help you develop productive relationships.

6. **You must not be discouraged in your job search.** You will succeed if you have a positive self-image and a *"can do"* attitude, and if you approach your job search with the under-

standing that rejections and disappointments are a normal part of the process. When you get discouraged, talk to positive people and think about this person: *"He dropped out of grade school. Ran a country store. Went broke. Took 15 years to pay off his bills. Took a wife. Unhappy marriage. Ran for the House. Lost twice. Ran for the Senate. Lost twice. Delivered speech that become a classic. Audience indifferent. Attacked daily by the press and despised by half the country. Despite all of this, imagine how many people all over the world have been inspired by this awkward, rumpled, brooding man who signed his name simply A. Lincoln."* As he and many other people demonstrate each day, persistence and determination centered around achieving specific goals do pay off.

These prerequisites are further explained and detailed as part of a set of 20 "principles" for job search success in Chapter Four.

The remaining chapters examine individual job search steps and provide information on how to:

- identify your motivated abilities and skills (MAS)
- develop a functional job objective
- write a resume for jobs outside education
- research organizations, individuals, and communities
- prospect, network, and conduct informational interview
- interview for jobs
- negotiate salary and benefits

CHOOSE THE RIGHT RESOURCES

We wish you well as you take this journey into this exciting and sometimes confusing world of self-discovery and action. We are primarily concerned with taking you through the most critical stages of a job search. These steps also are outlined in our other books: *Discover the Right Job For You!, Careering and Re-Careering for the 1990s, High Impact Resumes and Letters, Dynamite Resumes, Dynamite Cover Letters, Interview for Success, Network Your Way to Job and Career Success,* and *Salary Success.* We also address particular job and career fields in the following books: *The Complete Guide to Public Employment, Find a Federal Job Fast, The Complete Guide to International Jobs and*

Careers, The Almanac of American Government Jobs and Careers, and *The Almanac of International Jobs and Careers.* These and many other job search books are available directly from Impact Publications. For your convenience, you can order them by completing the order form at the end of this book or by acquiring a copy of the publisher's catalog.

Indeed, as a user of this book, you are entitled to a free copy of the most comprehensive career catalog available today—*"Jobs and Careers for the 1990s".* To receive the latest edition of this catalog of over 1,000 annotated job and career resources, write to:

IMPACT PUBLICATIONS
ATTN: Job/Career Catalog
4580 Sunshine Court
Woodbridge, VA 22192

They will send you a copy upon request. This 32-page catalog contains almost every important career and job finding resource available today, including many titles that are difficult if not impossible to find in bookstores and libraries. You will find everything from self-assessment books to books on resume writing, interviewing, government and international jobs, military, women, minorities, students, entrepreneurs as well as videos and computer software programs. This is an excellent resource for keeping in touch with the major resources that can assist you with every stage of your job search as well as with your future career development plans.

AUDIENCES AND USERS

This book is primarily designed for career anxious educators at the university, college, junior college, and secondary and elementary levels. Highly motivated to make a career change, these individuals should find this book most useful. At the same time, many satisfied and happy educators should learn a great deal from this book. We encourage them to read it, because in another 5 to 10 years they, too, may be interested in conducting a job search. It's best to know about your alternatives now than later.

Two types of educational administrators should find this book useful. Many administrators left teaching and research positions but now wish to advance their careers further by moving into administrative positions outside education. This book should help them make such a move. Other administrators are directing a retrenchment process of cutting budgets and releasing faculty. This book should help them develop outplacement programs for displaced faculty. Outplacement is an infinitely more humane and professional way of terminating personnel, and it benefits both employer and employee.

The final audience consists of would-be educators who are finishing college, graduate school, or leaving government or the private sector for colleges, universities, and schools. The strategies for getting out of education are also effective for getting into education. If you are graduating from college or beginning graduate school and contemplating an academic career, read this book along with other books on careers in education.

Individuals need to better plan and manage their careers. Educational jobs are a few of the career alternatives you may sample throughout your life. Like most alternatives, some educational jobs are good, some are bad, and most have their ups and downs. We wish you well in whatever you do, and hope the remaining chapters will make a significant difference in taking charge of your future. If there is only one thing you learn from this book, it is that if you choose, you *can* make a career change for the better. But you must plan and implement it properly. That's what this book is all about—making choices that result in achieving personal and professional goals.

Chapter Two

OLD MYTHS, NEW REALITIES, AND THE FUTURE

"What are the jobs, where are they found, and how do I get one?" Underlying these three frequently asked questions are certain assumptions about the careers of educators as well as the nature of jobs and today's job market. While such questions may anticipate easy answers, the answers are much more complex when examining the what, where, and how of alternative job opportunities for educators.

Let's answer these questions by first examining several myths that may impede your transition to jobs and careers outside education. These myths may affect your motivation and initiative by directing you into unproductive job search channels. Focusing on important employment issues affecting potential employees and employers, these myths also help clarify the best way to position yourself in today's job market.

A final question examines coming changes for jobs and careers: *"What are the major trends for jobs and careers in the 1990s?"* This chapter outlines several important changes that may affect your career plans in the decade ahead. Taken together, answers to these four questions should help you best focus your job search as you start it in the right direction.

MYTHS AND MUDDLERS

Many educators are unprepared and naive when looking for jobs outside education. Lacking experience in the non-educational job market, many educators tend to be *"job dumb"*. They muddle-through the job market with questionable perceptions of what it is, how it works, and how to make it responsive to their needs. Combining facts, stereotypes, myths, and folklore —gained from a mixture of logic, experience, and advice from well-meaning friends and relatives—these perceptions lead them down several unproductive paths. Such perceptions are often responsible for the self-fulfilling prophecy of the unsuccessful job seeker: *"There are no jobs available for me"*. For educators, this often translates into the feeling that *"Not many employers want to hire ex-educators"*.

> *Many job seekers . . . muddle-through the job market with questionable perceptions of how it works.*

EDUCATION AND EDUCATORS

Educators still believe several myths about education and the world of work outside education that affects how they approach jobs and careers both inside and outside education. Among the most prevalent such myths are the following:

MYTH 1:   **Jobs and salaries in public education will improve as more nontraditional students enroll in educational programs.**

REALITY: While many nontraditional students do participate in educational programs today, their numbers will not offset the losses of the traditional full-time equivalent students. Don't expect significant increases in such students in the coming decade. As important structural changes take place in education and training due to social and technological transformations, formal classroom training must increasingly compete with self-help video and computer training as well as telecourses which remove students from the traditional labor-intensive classroom where the jobs of educators are largely defined. Private industry, which spends over $40 billion a year on in-house education and training, will likely increase its programs as its skill needs become even more specialized in the decade ahead. Consequently, more and more education and training opportunities will be found in private industry rather than with public educational institutions. Such opportunities enable public educators to directly transfer many of their teaching skills to the corporate world of training.

MYTH 2: **The financing of education will improve significantly as education takes center stage on our national crisis agenda.**

REALITY: Despite political rhetoric to the contrary, financing education is extremely costly; it provides little political capital for politicians who must be sensitive to taxation and revenue questions and competing political interests. Educational issues will most likely receive greater media attention, but the gap between problems, promises, and performance will widen as scarce public resources continue to be allocated to other pressing issues that have more politically powerful constituents (i.e., elderly, minorities, poor). Maintenance of current obligations for education will become even more difficult as enrollments decline and costs increase. Since salaries and benefits are the largest expenditures in education, they will be a major target of cost-cutting measures. Major improvements in education are more likely to center around restructuring the traditional system of labor intensive classroom centered education with new technologies requiring fewer teachers and classrooms. Look for greater use of telecourses as one such measure. Unless the economy performs spectacularly, which is most unlikely, expect even leaner educational budgets in the coming decade.

MYTH 3: It's not a good idea to leave my position in education. If I wait another two or three years, things will get better.

REALITY: While wishful thinking may bring you some solace, chances are in another two or three years you will be two to three years further behind. The best time to make a move is when you feel sufficiently motivated to make the move by devoting the necessary time and effort to finding new employment outside education. If you procrastinate, you will go nowhere other than where you are at present.

The best time to make a move is when you feel sufficiently motivated to make the move.

MYTH 4: Educators cannot find jobs appropriate to their backgrounds outside education.

REALITY: Only if they look in the wrong places or view their skills in narrow academic discipline terms. Even in bad economic times, educators can find numerous alternative job opportunities. You must first think about marketing your *transferable talents* rather than your discipline or subject specialties. Your transferable talents are *skills* you already possess and readily use on your present job. As we will see in Chapter Five, you need to begin viewing your skills from a broader, more market-relevant perspective. For example, most high-level judgment jobs outside education stress the type of skills educators possess—analytical, communication, interpersonal, and leadership.

MYTH 5: I don't have the right skills for jobs outside education. I'll have to get another degree.

REALITY: While educators are great believers in the need for more education and training, they may or may not need more education for themselves when looking for employment outside education. You may quickly discover you have enough education—indeed, too much—for most jobs that interest you. Except in technical fields or those requiring certification, most jobs outside education require that you be first and foremost *trainable*—have the ability to acquire the knowledge, abilities, and skills necessary to perform well on a specific job as defined by an employer. You must have the *capacity* to learn, which is probably one of your major strengths. What additional training you will need will most likely be provided in-house by the employer. Therefore, one of your first tasks should be to take an inventory of the many skills you already possess. You need to be able to recognize these as your *strengths* and then *communicate* them clearly to potential employers. You need to assess your skills *before* even thinking about going back to school for more education and training. What you probably don't need is another degree!

Begin viewing your skills from a broader, more market-relevant perspective.

MYTH 6:   Employers don't want to hire ex-educators.

REALITY: While many employers have objections to hiring former educators—because of stereotypes about their work habits —you can and should overcome potential objections by projecting an image of a skilled, competent, loyal, and hard-working employee as well as by locating jobs appropriate for your particular mix of interests, abilities, skills, and goals. Some of the major objections include:

- Educators are too individualistic. They work in highly unstructured environments. Too used to *"doing their own thing"*, educators are not good at being part of a team and taking directions.

- Educators are not entrepreneurial; they seek individual gratification and self-esteem, are too preoccupied with impractical ideas, and lack a sense of good business.

- Educators lack a sense of productivity and accountability. Teachers perform routines rather than set goals and measure results. They are rewarded for seniority rather than for productivity.

- Educators lack pragmatism, practicality, and common sense. They are idealists who don't live in the real world of performance where profit and loss statements give meaning and direction to jobs, salaries, and benefits.

Like most stereotypes, there is some truth to these. Indeed, employers will point to examples of educators who couldn't make the transition to jobs outside education. More often than not, these stereotypes arise when former educators are misplaced in work environments that are not conducive to their motivational patterns and work styles. Many ex-educators find the wrong jobs for themselves and their employers. Therefore, you need to identify job opportunities outside education which are most appropriate for your pattern of motivated abilities and skills. We examine the nature of such patterns in Chapters Five, Six, and Seven.

MYTH 7:   **Money is not important to educators.**

REALITY: This myth provides a convenient rationale for not making much money in education. It is one reason why many educators are poorly paid and will continue to be so in the future. In fact, studies find that the most important correlate of job satisfaction among educators is money! And money becomes more important to educators the longer they stay in education and incur the increased costs of living attendant with supporting families and middle to upper-middle class lifestyles. There is nothing wrong in making a lot of money and enjoying it. Educators who leave education and double or triple their incomes seem to enjoy their work as well as their new-found salaries.

The most important correlate of job satisfaction among educators is money.

MYTH 8: I'll probably double or triple my income once I leave education.

REALITY: Maybe in the long-run, in another five or 10 years, but you may not initially experience a significant increase in income. However, you probably will not make less than what you do at present; some educators experience lower salaries at first. This is all part of the transition process. Once you establish a track record and get promoted, chances are you will increase your income substantially.

MYTH 9: Educational institutions are the most intellectually simulating environments to work in.

REALITY: It depends on which institution, school, department, or community you work and live in. Some have intellectually stifling environments. There are numerous challenging and stimulating environments outside education. For example, try living, working, and taking advantage of intellectual opportunities outside education in New York City, Washington, DC, San Francisco, and Los Angeles.

MYTH 10:   **Educational positions are the most secure, once you get tenure.**

REALITY: Tenure has been eroded by financial considerations. Elementary, secondary, and higher education institutions have learned how to reduce forces in spite of tenure. Security is when you are wealthy and have no superiors. As long as someone else pays your wages, your security is subject to the whims of your boss and the ups and downs of economic cycles. Educators may get three, six, or nine months notice before termination compared to the usual short-term notice outside education. Also, as long as educators remain relatively unorganized, they will lack security. The security of tenure also tends to keep salaries low and encourage deadwood. If your boss doesn't like you and you have tenure, he or she can always make your life miserable and thus get rid of you by other means: heavy teaching and advising loads, numerous and useless committee assignments, no promotions, insulting salary increments, no travel funds, or bad office location and space. The security and joys of tenure are more tenuous than many educators think or are willing to admit.

MYTH 11:   **Jobs outside education are more stressful and insecure.**

REALITY: It depends on the job. Many educators already work at jobs that are increasingly stressful and insecure. The problems of insecurity can be overcome by developing the ability to change jobs and careers when necessary with the minimum of down-time between jobs and employers. Stress is a more a function of how one deals with the work environment rather than how the work environment affects the individual. You can choose to establish your own stress level regardless of the particular job you perform.

MYTH 12:   **There are less politics in education than in other organizations.**

REALITY: Education probably has **more** politics due to the highly interpersonal nature of educational work. Politics in education can be just as vicious and debilitating as politics elsewhere. However, it differs in one major respect: in education politics often is played for **low stakes**. Elsewhere politics have greater meaning and impact and may be worth playing. Educators continue to fiercely compete for decreasing rewards. For example, in higher education big decisions often involve nickel-dime stakes which affect few people other than some petty players of academic politics. Academicians sometimes spend hours arguing in committee meetings over how to best divide $2,000 in travel funds among eight faculty members, or how to divide $5,000 in research money among 18 competing faculty members. On a larger scale, some national research funding groups attempt to allocate, for example, $60,000 to seven out of 80 competing academic research proposals. In such a situation, the question for many educators is: *"Can I really afford to play this game of high competition for low stakes?"*

Education probably has more politics due to the highly interpersonal nature of educational work.

MYTH 13: Educators have more freedom to *"do their own thing"*.

REALITY: Many educators have flexible time schedules, but unless they are deadwood, educators also have little free time to do their own thing. When they do have free time, they keep busy on job-related matters or work to supplement their incomes. Educators often follow Parkinson's Law: work expands to fill the time available for completion.

MYTH 14:   Educators have more status than professionals in other occupations.

REALITY: Maybe. At least many educators still believe this. However, you can't eat status; you can't take a trip on status; you can't buy a new home, car, or boat on status; and you can't send your kids to college on status. Worst of all, as educators enter the ranks of the working poor, their future social status is very much in doubt.

MYTH 15:   I don't know how to look for a job outside education.

REALITY: While you may be unfamiliar with the best methods and strategies for finding jobs, chances are you already possess the necessary job search skills to make an excellent transition. Most of these skills involve planning, organizing, conducting research, communicating, and networking. You'll learn to develop and relate these skills to a well organized job search in the following chapters.

MYTH 16:   I must give up my lifestyle when I leave education.

REALITY: You may or may not. More importantly, your lifestyle may change for the better since your income should increase substantially and thus allow you to do many things you dreamt of or never thought of doing. Once you leave education, you may quickly discover that you didn't have such a great lifestyle after all.

MYTH 17:   Ex-educators are likely to be offered lower salaries than other job candidates.

REALITY: This can happen if you let employers take advantage of you by using your last salary in education as the base for computing a salary offer. You should always stress your *value* to employers in terms of what both you and the position are worth. You do this by learning to negotiate a salary based upon performance considerations.

MYTH 18:   Educators are not good in sales positions.

REALITY: Educators are some of the best salespeople you will ever encounter. Their major strength is their ability to **communicate trust** and **teach** clients about a product or service rather than merely sell it based upon traditional sales techniques. The teaching orientation in sales tends to generate trust amongst potential buyers. You may discover that you are a terrific salesperson. By all means do not overlook sales positions because of negative stereotypes about what salespeople do.

MYTH 19: **It is unprofessional to use *"connections"* in getting a job, particularly in education.**

REALITY: Only ineffective job seekers believe this. Research shows that most educators got their jobs by using the ubiquitous *"connection"* indeed, as a group, academicians are major users of the *"ole boy network"*, *"connections"*, *"patron-client"* relations, and the informal system. Since educators' job hunting practices are similar to those of the general population, they should have little difficulty adapting their informal strategies to finding positions outside education. Indeed, many of the job search strategies outlined in this book will feel familiar to many educators.

MYTH 20: **Educators do not make good businesspeople nor entrepreneurs. It's best that they look for employment in government or with nonprofit organizations when they leave education.**

REALITY: While many educators lack an entrepreneurial orientation, this is more due to their extensive involvement with educational bureaucracies then to any inherent lack of business skills. Many educational institutions do not encourage and reward initiatives that may challenge the bureaucracy. On the other hand, many educators demonstrate a great deal of creativity, initiative, persistence, and tenacity in the process of pursuing degrees in higher education and in teaching courses. Creativity, initiative, persistence, and tenacity are important ingredients in business success. They lie at the heart of entrepreneurship.

All of these myths argue for changes in the perceptions and behavior of educators: they need to do more reality-testing with alternative jobs and careers than they have to date. In the absence of information on alternative realities, like other groups in society, educators tend to develop myths about their occupational benefits and importance vis-a-vis others. Once they learn about alternative jobs and careers outside education—and especially from individuals who have successfully made the transition—they discover a new world of jobs and careers that are both satisfying and rewarding.

JOBS AND CAREERS

Twelve additional myths often prevent individuals from being effective in finding a job in today's job market. These myths are equally applicable to educators who lack experience in finding jobs:

MYTH 21: **Anyone can find a job; all you need to know is how to find a job.**

REALITY: This *"form versus substance"* myth is often associated with career counselors who were raised on popular career planning exhortations of the 1970s and 1980s that stressed the importance of having positive attitudes and self-esteem, setting goals, dressing for success, and using interpersonal strategies for finding jobs. While such approaches may work well in an industrial society with low unemployment, they constitute myths in a post-industrial, high-tech society which requires employees to demonstrate both **intelligence and concrete work skills** as well as a **willingness to relocate** to new communities offering greater job opportunities. For example, many of today's unemployed are highly skilled in the old technology of the industrial society, but they live and own homes in economically depressed communities. These people lack the necessary **skills and mobility** required for getting jobs in high-tech, growth communities. Knowing job search skills alone will not help these people. Indeed, such advice and knowledge will most likely frustrate such highly motivated and immobile individuals who possess skills of the old technology.

The job market is highly decentralized, fragmented, and chaotic.

MYTH 22: The best way to find a job is to respond to classified ads, use employment agencies, and submit applications to personnel offices.

REALITY: Except for certain types of organizations, such as government, these formal application procedures are not the most effective ways of finding jobs. Such approaches assume the presence of an organized, coherent, and centralized job market—but no such thing exists. The job market is highly decentralized, fragmented, and chaotic. Classified ads, employment agencies, and personnel offices tend to list low paying yet highly competitive jobs. Most of the best jobs—high level, excellent pay, least competitive—are neither listed nor advertised; they are most likely found through word-of-mouth. When seeking employment outside education, your most fruitful strategy will be to conduct research and informational interviews on what career counselors call the *"hidden job market"*.

MYTH 23: Few jobs are available for me in today's competitive job market.

REALITY: This may be true if you lack marketable skills and insist on applying for jobs listed in newspapers, employment agencies, or personnel offices. Competition in the advertised job market usually is high, especially for jobs requiring few skills. Numerous jobs with little competition are available on the hidden job market. Jobs requiring advanced technical skills often go begging. Little competition may occur during periods of high unemployment, because many people quit job hunting after a few disappointing weeks of working the advertised job market.

MYTH 24:   **I know how to find a job, but opportunities are not available for me.**

REALITY: Most people don't know how to find a job, or they lack marketable job skills. They continue to use ineffective job search methods. Opportunities are readily available for individuals who understand the structure and operation of the job market, have appropriate work-content skills, and use job search methods designed for the hidden job market.

If you can define employers' needs as your skills, you might end up in the driver's seat!

MYTH 25:   **Employers are in the driver's seat; they have the upper-hand with applicants.**

REALITY: Most often no one is in the driver's seat. Not knowing what they want, many employers make poor hiring decisions. They frequently let applicants define their hiring needs. If you can define employers' needs as your skills, you might end up in the driver's seat!

MYTH 26:   **Employers hire the best qualified candidates. Without a great deal of experience and numerous qualifications, I don't have a chance.**

REALITY: Employers hire people for all kinds of reasons. Most rank experience and qualifications third or fourth in their pecking order of hiring criteria. Employers seldom hire the best qualified candidate, because *"qualifications"* are difficult to define and measure. Employers normally seek people with the following characteristics: competent, intelligent, honest, and likeable. *"Likeability"* tends to be an overall concern of employers. Employers want *value* for their money. Therefore, you must communicate to employers that you are such a person. You must overcome employers' objections to any lack of experience or qualifications. But never volunteer your weaknesses. The best qualified person is the one who knows how to get the job—convinces employers that he or she is the *most* desirable for the job.

If you go after a growth field, you will try to fit into a job rather than find a job fit for you.

MYTH 27: It is best to go into a growing field where jobs are plentiful.

REALITY: Be careful in following the masses to the *"in"* fields. First, many so-called growth fields can quickly become no-growth fields, such as aerospace engineering, nuclear energy, and defense contracting. Second, by the time you acquire the necessary skills, you may experience the *"disappearing job"* phenomenon: too many people did the same thing you did and consequently glut the job market. Third, since many people leave no-growth fields, new opportunities may arise for you. Fourth, if you go after a growth field, you will try to fit into a job rather than find a job fit for you. If you know what you do well and enjoy doing (Chapters Five, Six, and Seven), and what additional training you may need, you should look for a job or career conducive to your particular mix of skills, interests, and motivations. In the long-run you will be much happier and more productive finding a job fit for you.

MYTH 28: **People over 40 have difficulty finding a good job.**

REALITY: Yes, if they apply for youth jobs. Age should be an insignificant barrier to employment if you conduct a well organized job search and are prepared to handle this potential negative with employers. Age should be a positive and must be communicated as such. After all, employers want experience, maturity, and stability. People over 40 generally possess these qualities. As the population ages and birth rates decline, older individuals should have a much easier time changing jobs and careers.

MYTH 29: **I must be aggressive in order to find a job.**

REALITY: Aggressive people tend to be offensive and obnoxious people. Try being purposeful, persistent, and pleasant in all of your job search efforts. Such behavior is well received by potential employers!

MYTH 30: **I should not change jobs and careers more than once or twice. Job-changers are discriminated against in hiring.**

REALITY: While this may have been generally true 30 years ago, it is no longer true today. America is a skills-based society: individuals market their skills to organizations in exchange for money and position. Furthermore, since most organizations are small businesses with limited advancement opportunities, careers quickly plateau for most people. For them, the only way up is to get out and into another organization. Therefore, the best way to advance careers in a society of small businesses is to change jobs frequently. Job-changing is okay as long as such changes demonstrate career advancement. Most individuals entering the job market today will undergo several career and job changes regardless of their initial desire for a one-job, one-career life plan.

MYTH 31: **People get ahead by working hard and putting in long hours.**

REALITY: Success patterns differ. Many people who are honest, work hard, and put in long hours also get fired, have ulcers, and die young. Some people get ahead even though they are dishonest and lazy. Others simply have good luck or a helpful patron. Moderation in both work and play will probably get you just as far as the extremes. Chapter Four outlines some realistic ways to become successful in addition to hard work and long hours.

MYTH 32: **I should not try to use contacts or connections to get a job. I should apply through the front door like everyone else. If I'm the best qualified, I'll get the job.**

REALITY: While you may wish to stand in line for tickets, bank deposits, and loans—because you have no clout—standing in line for a job is dumb. Every employer has a front door as well as a back door. Try using the back door if you can. It works in many cases. Chapter Eleven outlines in detail how you can develop your contacts, use connections, and enter *both* the front and back doors.

REALITY AND THE PH.D. CABBIE

Many of these myths, along with the reality of leaving education, are perhaps best synthesized with the story of the Ph.D. cabbie. First published in 1980 in response to the career difficulties facing thousands of higher educators, it remains relevant for numerous educators in the 1990s who are likely to discover—like the Ph.D. cabbie—that life is indeed full of surprises:

The Ph.D. Cabbie: "I Don't Miss It, Not Anymore"

It was only a 10-block walk to the convention center, but the rain changed my mind about exercise. I climbed in a cab at the hotel entrance, gave my destination, and settled back. We didn't move. Cars jammed the streets in the morning rush hour.

"You with the teachers' convention?" the cabbie asked over the noise of slapping windshield wipers. I nodded at the eyes in the rearview mirror.

"Used to be a teacher myself."

"Is that right?" I smiled, more interested in watching the umbrellas play bumper car along the sidewalk.

"Yeah. Lasted about four years." He nosed the cab into traffic and hit the first of several halts before the end of the block.

"Why'd you quit?"

"I didn't. I was squeezed out in the money crunch. Things got a bit tight at ol' Plimpton College."

"College? You have a doctorate?"

"Yeah, Indiana. Class of '74."

"No kidding. How long you been driving a hack?"

"About six months."

Unemployment Abounds

"The way things are going, I might be joining you. A lot of underemployed Ph.D's running around."

"Underemployed? Yeah, well, I'm fully employed."

"I don't think I'd be happy not teaching."

"It's all relative. I'm happy when I'm feeding my family."

"I guess." I looked at my watch. *"I'm due to speak in about 20 minutes. Think I'll make it?"*

"You'll make it. This jam won't last much longer."

I watched the rain squiggle down the side window. Different openings for my speech ran through my mind. Maybe I should start with a reference to the weather.

"I don't miss it, not anymore," he began again. *"I never could get used to grading people."*

"Really? Haven't you tried to find another teaching job?"

"I did at first. Hell, I sent letters all over the place. All I ever got were polite responses requesting a pound of documentation."

"I finally figured it out: games. It's all who you know."

"Well, you're probably right." In fact, I *knew* he was right. I had gotten my job through the chairman of my doctoral committee.

"I didn't know anybody."

"Must have been rough."

"I won't bore you with the details. My wife made enough for us to get along, but the old lifestyle went out the window. One day I ran across an old friend and he got me this job."

"Doesn't sound like a long-term solution, though," I said.

"I have to admit one thing. I do miss the spotlight. As a professor you are somebody. It's an incredible high. Like with you, now — going to a conference, giving a speech, earning the praise. I loved that part. When I think of it, I forget all the hassles—the committee doldrums, the paperwork, the grades, even the publish-or-perish junk."

"I don't mind all that stuff. Helping students learn is what it's really all about —watching them develop, seeing them put ideas to work. It's worth it."

"Well, that, too, I guess. But being content is the big factor, no matter what you do."

Life 'No Five-year Plan'

"I know," I said. *"I sure enjoy what I do. I think most people enjoy their work —or they don't stick around long. It's got to be meaningful."*

"It gets meaningful when you can eat. The rest is pride. I had to work that out. I saw myself as a breed apart—officially registered by my Ph.D. I had to learn."

"But you're wasting years of training."

"Maybe. Maybe not. Life's not a five-year plan. And, hell, it's really not too bad driving. You meet some weirdos, but most of the time people are a riot."

"Must be a shock when they learn you're a Ph.D."

"Hey, I don't usually tell people. They'd think I was some kind of a nut. That's one of the first things you learn: Never tell anyone but an academic."

The traffic started to break.

"Think you'll ever teach again?"

"I doubt it. I don't think many teachers would go back if they knew it's less of a hassle outside—and the pay's better."

"For myself, I prefer summers off. I couldn't face the grind of a 9-to-5 job."

"That's a myth. You're working more than a 40-hour week—preparing for classes, grading papers, doing research.

"For sure."

"So there you are. Hey, I've got more time in this job that I ever had in teaching."

I caught sight of the convention center looming out of the rain. When we were directly across from the main entrance he pulled a quick U-turn and stopped at the curb.

"Good luck on your speech—and holding onto your job," he said as I paid. I tried to add a dollar tip, but he refused it. *"Keep it. You need it more than I do. I've already made last year's teaching salary in the few months I've been driving."*

'I'm a Survivor'

"No, take it. Think of it as a kind of rebate on your degree, compliments of my university." It just popped out.

He smiled. *"I'm a survivor. What the hell, life's full of surprises. Who knows? Maybe I've got a new teaching job already—right here in the driver's seat."*

I kept my dollar and went off through the rain. I found the room and took my place on the panel just as the first speaker began with a reference to the weather.

I opened with a story about my Ph.D. cabbie. People didn't know whether to laugh or take it seriously.

SOURCE: John D. Perron, "The Ph.D. Cabbie: 'I Don't Miss It, Not Anymore'." *The Chronicle of Higher Education* (August 25, 1980, p. 31).

FACING THE FUTURE

The future of education in the 1990s does not bode well for long-term careers in education. Indeed, education may well become a stepping-stone or career way-station for individuals who wish to immediately acquire work experience in schools and universities after graduation. These also tend to be the most productive years of educators' careers. Staying in education for four to seven years, many educators will then move on to jobs and careers outside education. Some may again return to education in their retirement years.

Many of the trends in education for the 1990s are continuations of trends begun in the late 1970s and early 1980s. They will once again become major issues in education due to the combination of financial and demographic changes:

- **Enrollments in elementary, secondary, and higher education will continue to decline** due to lower birth rates and fewer nontraditional students enrolling in educational programs.

- **Retrenchment and further cutbacks in elementary, secondary, and higher education** continue due to major financial crises in government at all levels combined with declining enrollments.

- **The security of tenure will be further eroded** as school districts and governing boards modify tenure policies in efforts to create greater flexibility to manage personnel during this period of retrenchment.

- **Salary inequities within education will widen** as schools and universities attempt to simultaneously deal with two competing problems: attract more teachers in high-demand subject areas with higher than average salaries and retain current teachers with salaries that barely keep up with annual rates of inflation.

As you plan your transition from education to other worlds of work, keep in mind the changing nature of the workforce and the workplace outside education in the years ahead. Stimulated by the larger demographic and technological changes taking place within society, 25 trends are emerging in the areas of job creation, youth, elderly, minorities, women, immigrants, part-time employment, service jobs, education and training, unions and labor-management relations, urban-rural shifts, regionalism, small businesses and entrepreneurship, and advancement opportunities. Together these changes point to both dangers and new opportunities in the job market for the decade ahead. The following trends constitute a quick primer for understanding the job markets of today and tomorrow:

TREND 1: Shortage of competent workers, with basic literacy and learning skills creates serious problems in developing an economy with an adequate work force for the jobs of the 90s.

Given the double-whammy of over 20 million functionally illiterate adults—or 1/6 of the potential labor force unable to read, write, or perform simple computations—and the availability of fewer easily trainable young entry-level workers, a large portion of the workforce is destined to remain at the lowest end of the job market despite the fact that over 15 million new jobs will be created in the 1990s. Most of these adults will remain permanently unemployed or underemployed while major labor shortages exist. As skill requirements rise rapidly for both entering and advancing within the workforce, the nation's economic development will slow due to the lack of skilled workers. Both public and private sector worker literacy, basic education, and training programs will continue to expand, but their contribution to improving the overall skill levels of the workforce is minimal. The American economy and workforce begin showing classic signs of Second and Third World economies—potential economic performance outstrips the availability of a skilled workforce.

TREND 2: A renewed and strong U.S. manufacturing sector will create few new jobs; service industries will be responsible for most job growth throughout the 1990s.

Despite popular notions of the *"decline"* of American manufacturing industries, these industries are following the model of American agriculture—increased productivity accompanied by the increased displacement of workers. American manufacturing industry is becoming one of the strongest economic sectors in terms of production output but the weakest sector in terms of its contribution to job growth the job creation. At the same time, American manufacturing is moving in the direction of Drucker's *"production sharing system"* by exporting the remaining high-cost, labor intensive aspects of the industries. As large manufacturing companies rebound in the 1990s by becoming productive with smaller and more highly skilled workforces, most new manufacturing jobs will develop among small manufacturing *"job shops"* employing fewer than 50 workers. The service industries, especially those in finance, retail, food, and health care, will continue to expand their workforces during the first half of the 1990s. The second half of the 1990s will witness major *"productivity"* and *"management"* improvement movements among service industries that developed among large manufacturing industries in the 1980s—a push for greater productivity because of (1) major labor shortages, and (2) the adaptation of new technology to increasingly inefficient, high-cost, labor intensive service industries, especially in the retail and health care industries.

TREND 3: **Unemployment remains high, fluctuating between a low of 5 percent and a high of 12 percent.**

These fluctuations are attributed to a combination of boom and bust cycles in the economy as well as the persistence of structural unemployment exacerbated by millions of functionally illiterate adults on the periphery of the economy.

TREND 4: **Government efforts to stimulate employment growth continues to be concentrated at the periphery of the job market.**

Most government programs aimed at generating jobs and resolving unemployment problems will be aimed at the poor and unskilled. These groups also are the least likely to relocate, use job search skills, develop standard work habits, or be trained in skills for tomorrow's job market. Given the mixed results from such programs and political pressures to experiment with some form of government-sponsored work-fare programs, the government finally develops programs to directly employ the poor and unskilled on government programs as well as contract-out this class of unemployed to government contractors who will provide them with education and training along with work experience.

TREND 5: **After difficult economic times during 1991 and 1992, the U.S. deficit finally declines in 1993 and trade becomes more balanced as the U.S. regains a more competitive international trade and debt position due to improved productivity of U.S. manufacturing industries and the devaluation of the U.S. dollar.**

International and domestic issues become closely tied to employment issues. Emphasis shifts to issues of unemployment, productivity, population growth, consumption, and regional conflicts in Third and Fourth World countries that threaten the stability of international markets and thus long-term employment growth in the U.S.

TREND 6: **A series of domestic and international crises—shocks and *"unique events"*, some that already occurred in the 1980s—emerge in the 1990s to create new boom and bust cycles contributing to high rates of unemployment.**

The most likely sources for the international crises will be problems developing amongst poor Third and Fourth World nations: energy and precious metals shortages due to a depletion of current stocks and regional military conflicts; the collapse of financial markets due to default on international debts; and dislocation of lucrative resource and consumption markets due to continued wars in the Middle East, South Africa, and South Asia. The most likely domestic crises center on financial markets, energy, water, and the environment. An energy crisis once again revitalizes the economies of Texas, Colorado, and Alaska. A new crisis—water shortages—in the rapidly developing Southwest, slows employment growth in the booming economies of Southern California and Arizona. Environmental issues, such as acid rain and water pollution, emerge as important international and domestic crises.

TREND 7:   New jobs will be created at the rate of 1 to 2 million each year, with some boom years resulting in the creation of more than 3 million jobs each year.

The good news is that employment will increase in most occupations throughout the 1990s. Economic expansion in the service sector, coupled with the low productivity and low cost of labor in many parts of the service sector, contributes over 90 percent of all new jobs. Large scale manufacturing experiences labor declines while small scale manufacturing *"job shops"* contribute most of the minimal job growth in the manufacturing sector. The labor declines will be offset by increases in related service jobs, especially in manufacturing sales and marketing.

TREND 8:   A major shortage of skilled craftspeople will create numerous production and service problems throughout the 1990s.

During the 1980s the number of apprenticeship programs declined significantly; fewer individuals received training in blue-collar occupations; and interest among the young in blue-collar trades declined markedly. The impact of these changes will be felt throughout the 1990s as production and service industries requiring critically skilled craftspeople experience major labor shortages. Expect to personally encounter the effects of these labor shortages—long waiting periods for servicing your automobile and for repairing your home and major appliances as well as very expensive charges for such services.

TREND 9:   As the baby-boomers reach middle age and as the birth-rate continues at a near zero-population growth rate, fewer young people will be available for entry-level positions during the 1990s.

Businesses will either recruit and train more of the hard-core unemployed, unskilled, and the elderly, and/or they will automate. As a result, more stopgap job opportunities will be available for individuals losing their jobs or wishing to change jobs or careers.

TREND 10: More job and career choices will be available for the elderly.

As the workforce increasingly ages, the trend toward early retirement will decrease. Many people will never retire, preferring instead part-time or self-employment in their later years. Others will retire from one job and then start new careers after age 50. Fewer social security benefits and higher costs of retirement will further transform retirement practices and systems throughout the 1990s. Expect to see more elderly working in the McDonald's and 7-Eleven stores of tomorrow.

TREND 11: More blacks and Hispanics, due to their dispropor-tionately high birth rates, low education and skill levels, poor economic status, and immigration, will enter the job market.

A large proportion of minorities will occupy the less skilled entry-level, service positions where they will exhibit marked language, class, and cultural differences. Upwardly mobile minorities may find advancement opportunities blocked because of the glut of relatively young supervisors, managers, and executives already in most organizations.

TREND 12: Women will continue to enter the labor market, accounting for over 60 percent female participation during the 1990s.

The entry of women into the workforce during the 1990s will be due less to the changing role of women than to the economic necessity of women to work in order to survive in an expensive consumer-oriented society. Women will account for two-thirds of the growth in all occupations.

They will continue to expand into non-traditional jobs, especially production and management positions. Both men and women in a growing number of two-career families will have the flexibility to change jobs and careers frequently.

TREND 13: More immigrants will enter the U.S.—both legally and illegally—to meet labor shortages at all levels.

Despite major efforts of the INS to stem the flow of illegal immigrants, labor market demands will require more immigrants to occupy low-paying, entry-level service jobs in the 1990s. The brain drain of highly skilled scientific and technical workers from developing countries to the U.S. will accelerate. Unskilled immigrants will move into service positions vacated by upwardly mobile Americans.

TREND 14: Part-time and temporary employment opportunities will increase.

With the increase in two-career families, the emergence of electronic cottages, and the smaller number of retirees, part-time and temporary employment will become a more normal pattern of employment for millions of Americans. More women, who wish to enter the job market but not as full-time employees, will seek new part-time employment opportunities. Temporary employment services will experience a boom in business as more and more companies attempt to lower personnel costs as well as achieve greater flexibility in personnel by hiring larger numbers of temporary employees.

TREND 15: White-collar employment will continue to expand in the fast growing service sector.

Dramatic growth in clerical and service jobs will take place in response to new information technology. The classification of workers into blue and white-collar occupations as well as into manufacturing and service jobs will become meaningless in a service economy dominated by white-collar workers.

TREND 16: **The need for a smarter workforce with specific technical skills will continue to impact on the traditional American education system with a demand for greater job market relevance in educational curriculum.**

Four-year colleges and universities will continue to face stable to declining enrollments as well as the flight of quality faculty to more challenging and lucrative jobs outside education. Declining enrollments will be due to the inability of these institutions to adjust to the educational and training skill requirements of the high-tech society as well as to the demographics of fewer numbers in the traditional 18-21 year-old student age population. The flight of quality faculty will be replaced by less qualified and inexpensive part-time faculty. Most community college, as well as specialized private vocational-technical institutions, will adapt to the changing demographics and labor market needs and flourish with programs most responsive to community employment needs. As declining enrollments, budgetary crises, and flight of quality faculty accelerates, many of the traditional four-year colleges and universities will attempt to shut down or limit the educational scope of community colleges in heated state political struggles for survival of traditional educational programs. More and more emphasis will be placed on providing efficient short-term, intensive skills training programs than on providing traditional degree programs—especially in the liberal arts. Career planning will become a major emphasis in education programs; a new emphasis will be placed on both specialization and flexibility in career preparation.

TREND 17: **Union membership will continue to decline as more blue-collar manufacturing jobs disappear and interest in unions wanes among both blue and white-collar employees.**

As unions attempt to survive and adjust to the new society, labor-management relations will go through a turbulent period of conflict, co-optation, and cooperation. Given declining union membership and the threat to layoff employees unless unions agree to give-back arrangements, unions will increasingly find themselves on the defensive, with little choice other than to agree to management demands for greater worker productivity. In the long-run, labor-management relations will shift from the traditional adversarial relationship to one of greater cooperation and participation of labor and management in the decision-making process. Profit sharing, employee ownership, and quality circles will become prominent features of labor-management relations which will contribute to the continuing decline, and eventual disappearance, of traditional unions in many industries. New organizational forms, such as private law firms specializing in the representation of employees' interests and the negotiation of employment contracts, will replace the traditional unions.

TREND 18: The population will continue to move into suburban and semi-rural communities as the new high-tech industries and services move in this direction.

The large, older central cities, especially in the Northeast and North Central regions, will continue to decline as well as bear disproportionate welfare and tax burdens due to their declining industrial base and deteriorating infrastructure. Cutbacks in their city government programs will require the retraining of public employees for private sector jobs. Urban populations will continue to move into suburban and semi-rural communities. Developing their own economic base, these communities will provide employment for the majority of local residents rather than serve as bedroom communities from which workers commute to the central city. With few exceptions, and despite noble attempts to *"revitalize"* downtown areas with new office, shopping, and entertainment complexes, most large central cities will continue to decline as their upwardly mobile residential populations move to the suburbs where the good jobs, housing, and education are found.

TREND 19: The population, as well as wealth and economic activity, will continue to shift into the Northwest, Southwest, and Florida at the expense of the Northeast and North Central regions.

By the year 2000 the South and West will have about 60 percent of the population. These areas will also be the home for the Nation's youngest population. Florida, Georgia, Texas, California, Arizona, and Washington will be the growth states of the 1990s; construction and local government in these states will experience major employment increases. Michigan, Ohio, Illinois, Indiana, and Pennsylvania will be in for continuing difficult times due to their declining industrial base, excessive welfare burdens, older population, and aging infrastructure. However, these same states may experience a strong recovery—based on the Massachusetts model of the 1980s—due to important linkages developing between their exceptionally well developed higher educational institutions and high-tech industries which depend on such institutions.

The growth regions also will experience turbulence as they see-saw between shortages of skilled labor, surpluses of unskilled labor, and urban growth problems. A *"unique event"*, such as a devastating earthquake in Southern California or major water shortages in California and Arizona could result in a sudden reversal of rapid economic and employment growth in the Southwest region.

The problems of the declining regions are relatively predictable: they will become an economic drain on the Nation's scarce resources; tax dollars from the growth areas will be increasingly transferred for nonproductive support payments. A new regionalism, characterized by numerous regional political conflicts, will likely arise centered around questions concerning the inequitable distribution of public costs and benefits.

TREND 20: The number of small businesses will continue to increase as new opportunities for entrepreneurs arise in response to the high-tech and service revolutions

and as more individuals find new opportunities to experiment with changing careers.

Over 700,000 new businesses will be started each year during the 1990s. These businesses will generate 90 percent of all new jobs created each year. The number of business failures will increase accordingly, especially during the bust cycles of the boom/bust economy. Increases in self-employment and small businesses will not provide many new opportunities for career advancement. The small promotion hierarchies of these businesses will help accelerate increased job-hopping and career changes. This new entrepreneurship is likely to breed greater innovation, competition, and productivity.

The best employment opportunities . . .
will be found among growing
companies employing fewer
than 2,500 employees.

TREND 21: As large companies continue to cut back, major job growth will take place among small companies and millions of new start-up businesses.

The best employment opportunities in terms of challenges, salaries, and advancement opportunities will be found among growing companies employing fewer than 2,500 employees but more than 100 employees. The large Fortune 1000 companies will continue to cut back personnel as they attempt to survive intense competition by becoming more productive through the application of new technology to the workplace and through the introduction of more efficient management systems. Cutbacks will further lower the morale of remaining employees who will seek new job and career opportunities.

TREND 22: Opportunities for career advancement will be increasingly limited within most organizations.

Organizations will have difficulty providing career advancement for employees due to (1) the growth of small businesses with short advancement hierarchies, (2) the postponement of retirement, (3) the continuing focus on nonhierarchical forms of organization, and (4) the already glutted managerial ranks. In the future, many of today's managers will have to find nonmanagerial positions. Job satisfaction will become less oriented toward advancement up the organizational ladder and more toward such organizational perks as club memberships, sabbaticals, vacations, retraining opportunities, flexible working hours, and family services.

TREND 23: Job satisfaction will become a major problem as many organizations will experience difficulty in retaining highly qualified personnel.

Greater competition, fewer promotions, frustrated expectations, greater discontent, and job-hopping will arise in executive ranks due to limited advancement opportunities. Managerial and executive turnover will increase accordingly. The problem will be especially pronounced for many women and minorities who have traditional aspirations to advance to the top but will be blocked by the glut of managers and executives from the baby-boom generation. Many of these frustrated individuals will initiate affirmative action cases to open the closed upper ranks as well as become entrepreneurs by starting their own businesses in competition with their former employers.

TREND 24: Many employers will resort to new and unorthodox hiring practices and improved working conditions in order to recruit and retain critical personnel.

In an increasingly tight job market for skilled workers, employers will use new and more effective ways of finding and keeping personnel; job fair weekends; headhunters and executive search firms; temporary employment services; raids of competition's personnel; bonuses to present employees for finding needed personnel; entry-level bonuses for new recruits; attractive profit-sharing packages for long-term commitments; vacation and travel packages; relocation and housing services; flex-time and job-sharing; home-based work; and day care services.

TREND 25: **Job-hopping will Increase as more and more individuals learn how to change careers.**

As more job and career opportunities become available for the skilled and savvy worker, as pension systems become more portable, and as job search and relocation techniques become more widely known, more and more individuals will change jobs and careers in the 1990s. The typical employee will work in one job and organization for four years and then move on to a similar job in another organization. Within 12 years this individual will have acquired new interests and skills and thus decide to change to a new career. Similar four and 12-year cycles of job and career changes will be repeated by the same individual. Job-hopping will become an accepted and necessary way of getting ahead in the job and career markets of tomorrow.

The combination of myths and predictions for the future identify most of the major employment issues facing educators in the 1990s. Assuming you are sufficiently motivated at this point to make a career change, let's explore some alternative jobs and careers for educators as well as specify the most important how-to strategies for making the transition from education to other worlds of work.

Chapter Three

ALTERNATIVE JOBS AND CAREERS

If you've spent all of your worklife in education, you may have little idea of what you are best qualified to do outside education. Indeed, your academic degrees were in specific subject areas that you, in turn, learned to teach to students. You may wonder what types of employers outside education want to hire someone with your academic specialty?

Educators are increasingly learning that they are talented to do many things outside education. They quickly discover they have knowledge, skills, and abilities that employers readily seek. However, it is their skills and abilities rather than their subject matter knowledge that employers find most attractive. Identifying and positioning these skills in relation to alternative jobs and careers will occupy a great deal of your job search time.

SUCCESSFUL TRANSITIONS

Thousands of educators make successful career transitions each year. They do so by marketing their skills in a variety of occupational areas rather than into only education-relevant careers, such as corporate education and training programs. Ex-educators are well represented across occupational spectrums, from insurance agents and advertising directors to city managers and corporate executives. What they all seem to have in common is the ability to use the many skills they acquired in education in diverse occupational settings. Their most important skills appear to be their ability to organize, communicate, and create.

Fran Bastress, studying 21 teachers who made successful career transitions (*Teachers in New Careers*), discovered that these ex-educators shared four major characteristics:

- **Took risks and sacrificed:** Most realized they had to give up something if they wanted to gain something else. They were prepared to leave a work world they knew and had control over (classroom) for one that was uncertain and largely uncontrolable.

- **Acquired the necessary work-content skills required in new career fields:** While many knew they had important transferable skills, they also realized they needed to acquire new skills for jobs outside education. Many used their spare time as teachers to learn new skills. They did this through summer and part-time experience, temporary and part-time jobs, professional development programs, course work, degree programs, independent study, internships, volunteer experience, self-employment, and avocations.

- **Used networking strategies for landing new jobs:** Most discovered the importance of penetrating the hidden job market through the use of networking strategies that enabled them to gather important job information and referrals as well as open the doors of potential employers.

- **Persisted in making the change and were determined to achieve their goals:** In the end, persistence, determination, and tenacity paid off. Highly motivated to make a career change, they persisted in pursuing their goals. Although they experienced rejections, disappointments, and frustrations, they simply did not give up.

What most of these ex-teachers learned is that there were no one or two careers they were best suited for because of their backgrounds in education. Instead, they had to assess their interests, abilities, and skills and then link them to different jobs and careers that were most appropriate for them. Finding the right job *"fit"* took time and effort.

EXPLORING ALTERNATIVES

Many educators think of their job qualifications as being their discipline or subject matter. When they look outside education, they have difficulty aligning their subject matter with specific non-teaching jobs. For example, what can a teacher do with a degree in history, sociology, political science, English, education, or anthropology? Other disciplines may be more easily transferred outside education. We know teachers in business, economics, chemistry, physics, law, medicine, engineering, and art can more easily transfer their subject knowledge and skills to jobs in government and business. But what about others who are less certain of the relevance of their academic training to the nonacademic world?

Teachers are often told they should pursue jobs in several occupational fields that seem to be best suited for their skills. In fact, a few books have been written for teachers that are basically summaries of alternative job and career fields for educators. Based more on a simple logic of aligning the seeming interests and skills of educators with job descriptions of educator-related occupations than on data about what ex-educators actually do once they leave education, the following alternative job and career fields are frequently presented to educators as their potential new worlds of work. These occupations constitute a kind of *"revolving door"* for educators who never really leave education—only move across the street where they can pursue education in other more financially rewarding organizational settings:

- **Training and development:** Involves curriculum planning and classroom teaching activities; this is truly education in a different organizational setting.

- **Publishing and technical writing:** Involves research, writing, communication, and organization skills; closely linked to educational institutions which constitute a major market for their products.

- **Computers:** Includes a variety of occupational and technical skill areas, such as programming, consulting, technical writing, training, publishing, servicing, marketing, and sales.

- **Human resources and personnel:** Involves interviewing, recruiting, training, counseling, consulting, planning, and processing of forms.

- **Public relations:** Emphasizes strong communication, interpersonal, sales, and organizational skills.

- **Media:** Television, radio, video, magazines, and newspapers. Involves planning, organizational, research, analytical, and communication skills in quick-paced decision-making settings.

- **Sales and account executives:** Involves skills normally associated with selling products and services—organization, presentation, communication, persuasion, and interpersonal. Selling style of educators tends to be a real plus for businesses: educators tend to *teach* clients about products and services rather than persuade them through traditional motivational sales techniques. Ex-educators make some of the best real estate, insurance, travel, advertising, and automobile salespeople. They also make good stock brokers and employment recruiters.

- **Government employee:** With more than 10 million federal, state, and local government employees in positions outside education, the number of job opportunities appropriate for educators is infinite—from national security positions to public welfare administration positions. Many tend to gravitate toward education administrative positions in local education bureaucracies, state departments of education, and the U.S. Department of Education.

- **Associations, nonprofit organizations, and foundations:** Over 150,000 such organizations provide numerous job opportunities relevant to educators. Many of these organizations primarily focus on education issues. They are disproportionately headquartered in Washington, DC, New York City, and Chicago. Others provide exciting job opportunities in policy areas of considerable interest to educators—child care, labor, poverty, race, health care, elderly, criminal justice, women, minorities, housing, transportation, and real estate. Jobs involve everything from research, publishing, and training to public relations and lobbying activities. Many organizations function in both the domestic and international arenas and thus offer excellent opportunities to travel and work abroad.

Many ex-educators also become accountants, librarians, business administrators, social workers, editors, hospital administrators, musicians, bookkeepers, secretaries, legal aides, bankers, and social welfare supervisors. Many also start their own businesses based upon the skills and interests they acquired while in education. Some of the most popular businesses involve consulting and training.

> *Educators tend to demonstrate one*
> *dominant skill pattern: the*
> *capacity to learn and adapt*
> *to new situations.*

While many educators have gone into the above fields, because of a seemingly close linkage between the skills of educators and the requirements of these fields, educators are also found pursuing successful careers in many other fields. The jobs and careers outlined thus far tend to be stereotypes of alternative careers for educators based upon a superficial view of their transferable skills: planning, organizing, communicating, initiating, and creating. There is no reason to believe such highly generalized skills are disproportionately distributed in favor of educators. These skills are in demand in most jobs and careers, and they are widely distributed throughout the general population. By all means do not limit your thinking to these alternatives alone, because they do not represent the reality of alternative jobs and careers for educators. In fact, educators go into hundreds of different occupations in addition to those already outlined. Above all, educators tend to demonstrate one dominant skill pattern: the capacity to learn and adapt to new situations. Persistence, determination, and tenacity also tend to be characteristics of many educators that serve them well in a variety of jobs and careers outside education.

What we do know is that educators have many marketable skills that are suitable for thousands of jobs. Studies show that educators tend to predominate in these skills areas because of their day-to-day work in education:

- Organizing things and people
- Problem solving
- Supervising/coordinating
- Initiating
- Communicating
- Writing
- Researching
- Analyzing/synthesizing
- Motivating/persuading
- Creating/designing new projects or systems
- Evaluating
- Leading
- Administering
- Delegating

Most of these skills easily transfer to thousands of jobs outside education. Indeed, many of these—especially communicating, problem solving, and analyzing—are employers' most sought after skills. These are major weaknesses in their workforces that they constantly need to resolve by either training existing employees or hiring individuals with these competencies.

At the same time, each educator possesses certain knowledge and technical skills (work-content skills) that may or may not be directly transferred to jobs and careers outside education. In the process of assessing your skills and abilities, you should determine whether or not you have sufficient knowledge and skills to pursue the jobs that most interest you. If not, you may need to consider acquiring new work-content skills to complement the many strong transferable skills you already possess.

JOB MATCHING

If you need to sensitize yourself to the many job and career alternatives available today, you may want to examine the following directories that describe different alternatives; some identify interests that may be most compatible with each alternative:

- **The Occupational Outlook Handbook** (U.S. Department of Labor). This massive directory is the *"bible"* for identifying over 20,000 job titles. Each job is annotated, organized by major job categories, and cross-referenced by industry and title.

- **Occupational Outlook Handbook** (U.S. Department of Labor). Published biannually, this is the standard sourcebook on over 200 of America's most popular careers. Provides clear descriptions of each job, including working conditions, educational and training requirements, salaries, and future prospects.

- **Encyclopedia of Careers and Vocational Guidance**, 4 Volumes (J. G. Ferguson Co.). Newly revised (1990) this standard reference examines hundreds of technical and high-tech occupations in addition to the standard career and job fields. Vol 1: *Industry Profiles*; Vol. 2: *Professional Careers*; Vol. 3: *Specific and General Careers*; Vol. 4: *Technicians Careers*.

- **The Guide for Occupational Exploration** (National Forum Foundation). Based on the U.S. Department of Labor research, this guide lists more than 20,000 jobs by occupational cluster, skills required, job title, and industry groups. This is the key book that provides some analytical substance to the **Dictionary of Occupational Titles** and the **Occupational Outlook Handbook**.

Several computerized programs also provide information on alternative jobs and careers appropriate for people with particular skill and interest profiles. The most popular, comprehensive, and powerful programs are the **Discover II** and **Sigi-Plus**. Both programs assist users in identifying their skills and interests and then matching them with appropriate jobs. Both programs are widely used in career and counseling centers at community colleges as well as four-year colleges and universities. Even if you are not a student, you should be able to get access to these programs through your local community college. You might also check with your local high school, women's center, or library for information on the availability of these excellent assessment programs.

Several other computerized job matching programs are also available. In particular, look for the following:

- *Computerized Career Assessment and Planning Program*
- *Computerized Career Information System*
- *The Micro Guide to Careers Series*

DO FIRST THINGS FIRST

When planning a job or career change, it's best to do first things first. And the first thing you do *not* want to do is identify alternative jobs and careers you think look interesting. These may be fantasies that have no relation to the transferable and work-content skills you already possess. Instead, you should first familiarize yourself with your particular mix of interests, abilities, and skills to determine if indeed you have the requisite motivational pattern to pursue certain jobs and careers. You do this by addressing three interrelated questions:

- What do I do well? (your abilities and skills)

- What do I enjoy doing? (your interests and values)

- What do I want to do in the future that best incorporates what
  I do well and enjoy doing? (your goals)

Once you assess what it is you do well and enjoy doing and then reformulate this information into a clear objective centered around alternative jobs and careers best suited to your pattern of motivated abilities and skills (MAS), you will be well prepared to uncover the best job and career alternatives for you. As part of the critical self-assessment process, you will eventually match your MAS with alternative jobs and careers that appear to be the most appropriate *"fit"* for your MAS. This process is best illustrated in the diagram on page 61. It outlines how your interests, values, abilities, and skills are related to alternative jobs and careers.

FIND THE RIGHT JOB PROCESS

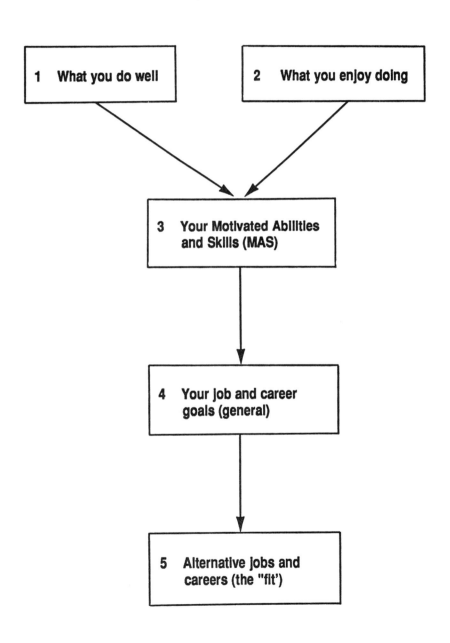

BEST ALTERNATIVES

The best job and career alternative for you is when *you* decide what it is you want to do (set goals) and develop an intelligent plan of action that links your interests, values, abilities, skills, and goals to job alternatives. You do this by going through a well organized career development and job search process that ultimately focuses on these alternatives.

Your goal should be to find a job
fit for you rather than try to
fit yourself into a job that
looks interesting.

The remaining chapters show you how to organize yourself for success in today's challenging job market by first identifying your motivated abilities and skills, developing an objective, and then targeting your job search on specific jobs and careers that are most appropriate for you. In other words, the methods are designed to discover the *"unique you"* which consists of a particular mix of interests, values, abilities, skills, and goals that are the basis for motivating you in specific work settings. You first need to know your pattern of motivated abilities and skills *before* identifying alternative jobs and careers best suited for your MAS. You will discover the best job for you is one that clearly fits into your pattern of motivated abilities and skills.

In the end, your goal should be to find a job fit for you rather than try to fit yourself into a job that looks interesting or is available. If you do this, your transition to new jobs and careers outside education can be most rewarding.

Chapter Four

ORGANIZE FOR SUCCESS

Doing first things first requires some basic self-knowledge about your capabilities to conduct an effective job search. Do you, for example, know what your major strengths are and how to communicate them to potential employers outside education? Do you know which jobs are ideally suited for your particular skills and motivations? Can you develop a one to two-page resume—not a curriculum vita—that clearly communicates your qualifications to employers? How well can you plan and implement a job search that will lead to several interviews and a job offer that is right for you?

We need to first address these questions prior to examining your interests, values, abilities, skills, motivations, and goals as well as the job search skills that will enable you to make a career transition.

TEST YOUR CAREERING COMPETENCIES

Knowing *where* the jobs are is important to your job search. But knowing *how to find a job* is even more important. Before you acquire names, addresses, and phone numbers of potential employers, you should possess the necessary job search knowledge and skills for gathering and using job information effectively.

Answers to many of your job related questions are found by examining your present level of job search knowledge and skills. Successful job seekers, for example, use a great deal of information as well as specific skills and strategies for getting the jobs they want.

Let's begin by testing for the level of job search information, skills, and strategies you currently possess as well as those you need to develop and improve. You can easily identify your level of job search competence by completing the following exercise:

──── YOUR CAREERING COMPETENCIES ────

INSTRUCTIONS: Respond to each statement by circling which number at the right best represents your situation.

> **SCALE:** 1 = strongly agree
> 2 = agree
> 3 = maybe, not certain
> 4 = disagree
> 5 = strongly disagree

1.	I know what motivates me to excel at work.	1 2 3 4 5
2.	I can identify my strongest abilities and skills.	1 2 3 4 5
3.	I have seven major achievements that clarify a pattern of interests and abilities that are relevant to my job and career.	1 2 3 4 5
4.	I know what I both like and dislike in work.	1 2 3 4 5
5.	I know what I want to do during the next 10 years.	1 2 3 4 5
6.	I have a well defined career objective that focuses my job search on particular organizations and employers.	1 2 3 4 5
7.	I know what skills I can offer employers in different occupations outside education.	1 2 3 4 5
8.	I know what skills employers most seek in candidates.	1 2 3 4 5
9.	I can clearly explain to employers what I do well and enjoy doing.	1 2 3 4 5

10. I can specify why an employer should hire me.   1 2 3 4 5

11. I can gain support of family and friends for
    making a job or career change.   1 2 3 4 5

12. I can find 10 to 20 hours a week to conduct
    a part-time job search.   1 2 3 4 5

13. I have the financial ability to sustain a three-
    month job search.   1 2 3 4 5

14. I can conduct library and interview research
    on difficult occupations, employers, organizations,
    and communities.   1 2 3 4 5

15. I can write different types of effective resumes,
    job search letters, and thank-you notes.   1 2 3 4 5

16. I can produce and distribute resumes and
    letters to the right people.   1 2 3 4 5

17. I can list my major accomplishments in
    action terms.   1 2 3 4 5

18. I can identify and target employees I want to
    interview.   1 2 3 4 5

19. I can develop a job referral network.   1 2 3 4 5

20. I can persuade others to join in forming a job
    search support group.   1 2 3 4 5

21. I can prospect for job leads.   1 2 3 4 5

22. I can use the telephone to develop prospects and
    get referrals and interviews.   1 2 3 4 5

23. I can plan and implement an effective direct-mail
    job search campaign.   1 2 3 4 5

24. I can generate one job interview for every 10 job
    search contacts I make.   1 2 3 4 5

25. I can follow-up on job interviews.   1 2 3 4 5

26. I can negotiate a salary 10-20% above what an
    employer initially offers.   1 2 3 4 5

27. I can persuade an employer to renegotiate my
     salary after six months on the job.   1 2 3 4 5

28. I can create a position for myself in an organization. 1 2 3 4 5

                                    TOTAL _____

You can calculate your overall careering competencies by adding the numbers you circled for a composite scale. If your total is more than 75 points, you need to work on developing your careering skills. How you scored each item will indicate to what degree you need to work on improving specific job search skills. If your score is under 50 points, you are well on your way toward job search success. In either case, this book should help you better focus your job search as well as identify job search skills you need to acquire or strengthen.

FINDING JOBS BY PLAN

Finding the right job requires that you (1) know who you are, (2) where you want to go, and (3) how to get there. This involves an important process of moving from an initial stage of self-awareness to several other action stages involving specific job search activities that eventually result in employment.

If you have a clear understanding of the relationship of each element within this process, you should be in a better position to know who you are and where you want to go. The process becomes a crucial blueprint revealing how to get where you want to go.

As you plan your career change, you will join millions of individuals who do so each year. Indeed, more than 15 million people find themselves unemployed each year. Millions of others try to increase their satisfaction within the workplace as well as advance their careers by looking for alternative jobs and careers. If you are like most workers, you will make more than 10 job changes and between 3 and 5 career changes during your lifetime.

But how do you make such changes? Do you look for jobs in a well thought-out and planned manner, or do new jobs come to you by accident? Most people make job or career transitions by accident. They do little other than take advantage of opportunities that may arise unexpectedly.

While chance and luck do play important roles in finding employment, we recommend that you *plan* for future job and career changes so that you will experience even greater degrees of chance and luck!

Finding a job or changing a career in a systematic and well-planned manner is hard yet rewarding work. The task should first be based on a clear understanding of the key ingredients that define jobs and careers. Starting with this understanding, you should next convert key concepts into action steps for implementing your job search.

A career is a series of related jobs which have common skill, interest, and motivational bases.

A career is a series of related jobs with common skill, interest, and motivational bases. You may change jobs several times without changing careers. But once you change skills, interests, and motivations, you change careers. Teachers, for example, who move from the classroom to an educational administrative position only change jobs within education; their career track rather than career changes. They change careers once they leave the field of education.

It's not easy to find a job given the present structure of the job market. You will find the job market to be relatively disorganized, although it projects an outward appearance of coherence. If you seek comprehensive, accurate, and timely job information, the job market will frustrate you with its poor communication. While you will find many employment services ready to assist you, such services tend to be fragmented and their performance is often disappointing. Job search methods are controversial and many are ineffective.

No system is organized to give people jobs. At best you will encounter a *decentralized and fragmented system* consisting of job listings in newspapers, trade journals, employment offices, or computerized job data banks—all designed to link potential candidates with available job openings. Many people will try to sell you job information as well as questionable job search services, including testing and assessment exercises that you can easily do on your own with the help of this book! While efforts are underway to create a nationwide computerized job bank which would list available job vacancies on a daily basis, don't expect such data to become available soon nor to be very useful. Many of the listed jobs may be non-existent, at a low skill and salary level, or represent only a few employers. In the end, most systems organized to help you find a job do not provide you with the information you need in order to land the job that is most related to your interests and skills.

UNDERSTAND THE CAREER DEVELOPMENT PROCESS

Finding a job is both an art and a science; it encompasses a variety of basic facts, principles, and skills which can be learned but which also must be adapted to individual situations. Thus, *learning how to find a job* can be as important to career success as *knowing how to perform a job.* Indeed, job finding skills are often more important to career success than job performance or work-content skills.

Our understanding of how to find jobs and change careers is illustrated on pages 69 and 70. As outlined on page 69, you should involve yourself in a four-step career development process as you prepare to move from one job to another.

Job finding skills are often more important to career success than job performance or work-content skills.

FOUR STEP CAREER DEVELOPMENT PROCESS

1. Conduct a self-assessment:

This first step involves assessing your skills, abilities, motivations, interests, values, temperaments, experience, and

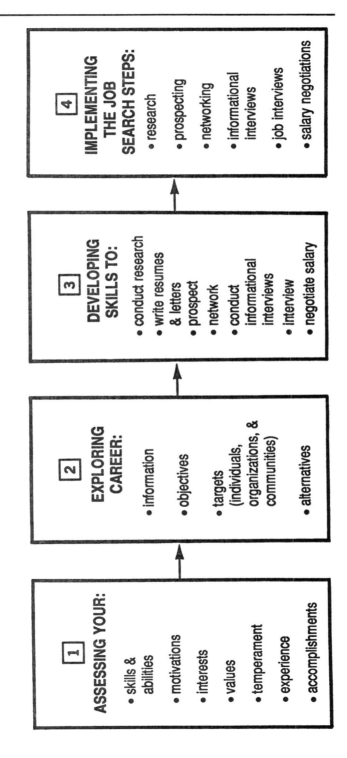

THE CAREER DEVELOPMENT PROCESS

1 **ASSESSING YOUR:**
- skills & abilities
- motivations
- interests
- values
- temperament
- experience
- accomplishments

2 **EXPLORING CAREER:**
- information
- objectives
- targets (individuals, organizations, & communities)
- alternatives

3 **DEVELOPING SKILLS TO:**
- conduct research
- write resumes & letters
- prospect
- network
- conduct informational interviews
- interview
- negotiate salary

4 **IMPLEMENTING THE JOB SEARCH STEPS:**
- research
- prospecting
- networking
- informational interviews
- job interviews
- salary negotiations

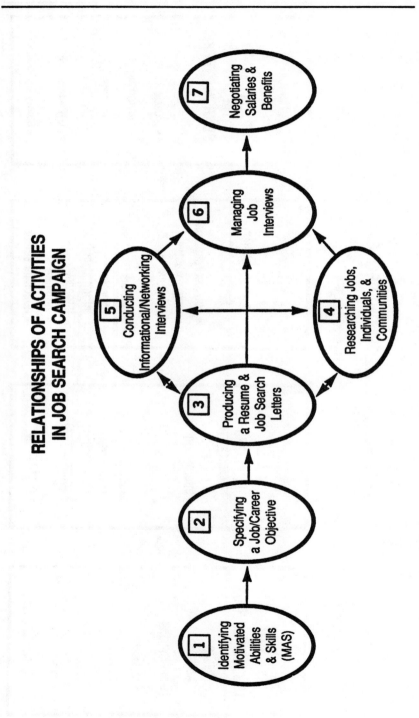

RELATIONSHIPS OF ACTIVITIES
IN JOB SEARCH CAMPAIGN

7 Negotiating Salaries & Benefits

6 Managing Job Interviews

5 Conducting Informational/Networking Interviews

4 Researching Jobs, Individuals, & Communities

3 Producing a Resume & Job Search Letters

2 Specifying a Job/Career Objective

1 Identifying Motivated Abilities & Skills (MAS)

accomplishments—the major concern of this book. Your basic strategy is to develop a firm foundation of information on **yourself** before proceeding to other stages in the career development process. This self-assessment develops the necessary self-awareness upon which you can effectively communicate your qualifications to employers as well as focus and build your career.

2. Gather career and job information:

Closely related to the first step, this second step is an exploratory, research phase of your career development. Here you need to formulate goals, gather information about alternative jobs and careers through reading and talking to informed people, and then narrow your alternatives to specific jobs.

3. Develop job search skills:

The third step focuses your career around specific job search skills for landing the job you want. As further outlined on page 69, these job search skills are closely related to one another as a series of *job search steps*. They involve conducting research, writing resumes and letters, prospecting and networking, conducting informational interviews, interviewing for a job, and negotiating salary and terms of employment. Each of these job search skills involves well-defined strategies and tactics you must learn in order to be effective in the job market.

4. Implement each job search step:

The final career development step emphasizes the importance of transforming understanding into *action*. You do this by implementing each job search step which already incorporates the knowledge, skills, and abilities you acquired in Steps 1, 2, and 3.

ORGANIZE AND SEQUENCE
YOUR JOB SEARCH

The figure on page 70 further expands our career development process by examining the key elements in a successful job search. It consists of a seven-step process which relates your past, present, and future. We will cover all of these steps in subsequent chapters.

Based on this concept, **your past** is well integrated into the process of finding a job or changing your career. Therefore, you should feel comfortable conducting your job search: it represents the best of what you are in terms of your past and present accomplishments as these relate to your present and future goals. If you base your job search on this process concept, you will communicate your **best self** to employers as well as focus on **your strengths** both during the job search and on the job.

Since the individual job search steps are interrelated, they should be followed in sequence. If you fail to properly complete the initial self-assessment steps, your job search may become haphazard, aimless, and costly. For example, you should never write a resume (Step 3) before first conducting an assessment of your skills (Step 1) and identifying your objective (Step 2). Relating Step 1 to Step 2 is especially critical to the successful implementation of all other job search steps. You **must** complete Steps 1 and 2 **before** continuing on to the other steps. Steps 3 to 6 may be conducted simultaneously because they complement and reinforce one another.

Try to sequence your job search as close to these steps as possible. The true value of this sequencing will become very apparent as you implement your plan.

The processes and steps identified on pages 69 and 70 represent the careering and re-careering processes used successfully during the past 30 years. They are equally relevant for educators in the 1990s.

You should also recognize the importance of acquiring work-content skills along with job search skills. In the job markets of today and tomorrow, you need to constantly review your work-content skills to make sure they are appropriate for the changing job market. Assuming you have the necessary work-content skills, you should be ready to target your skills on particular jobs and careers that you do well and enjoy doing. You will be able to avoid the trap of trying to fit into jobs that are not conducive to your particular mix of interests, abilities, skills, and motivations.

SEEK PROFESSIONAL
ASSISTANCE WHEN NECESSARY

While some people can successfully conduct a job search based on the advice of books such as this, many others also need the assistance of various professional groups that offer specific career planning and job search services. These groups offer everything from testing and assessment services to offering contacts with potential employers, including job vacancy information and temporary employment services. Some do one-on-one career counseling while others sponsor one to three-day workshops or six to twelve-week courses on the various steps in the career planning process. You should know something about these services before you invest your time and money beyond this and other career planning and job search books.

OPTIONS

You have two options in organizing your job search. First, you can follow the principles and advice outlined in this and many other self-directed books. Just read the chapters and then put them into practice by following the step-by-step instructions. Second, you may wish to seek professional help to either supplement or replace this book. Indeed, many people will read parts of this book—perhaps all of it—and do nothing. Unwilling to take initiative, lacking sufficient time or motivation, or failing to follow-through, many people will eventually seek professional help to organize and implement their job search. They will pay good money to get someone else to tell them to follow the advice found in this book. Some people need this type of expensive motivation.

At the same time, we recognize the value of professional assistance. Especially with the critical assessment and objective setting steps (Chapters Five, Six, and Seven), some individuals may need more assistance than our advice and exercises provide. You may, for example, want to take a battery of tests to better understand your interests and values in relation to alternative jobs and careers. And still others, due to a combination of job loss, failed relationships, or depression, may need therapy best provided by a trained psychologist or psychiatrist rather than career testing and information services provided by career counselors. If any of these situations pertain to you, by all means seek professional help.

You also should beware of pitfalls in seeking professional advice. While many services are excellent, other services are useless and fraudulent. Remember, career planning and job assistance are big businesses involving millions of dollars each year. Many people enter these businesses without expertise. Professional certification in these areas is extremely weak to non-existent in some states. Indeed, many so-called *"professionals"* get into the business because they are unemployed. In other words, they major in their own problem! Others are frauds and hucksters who prey on vulnerable and naive people who feel they need a *"specialist"* or *"expert"* to get them a job. They will take your money in exchange for broken promises. You will find several services promising to assist you in finding all types of jobs. You should know something about these professional services before you venture beyond this book.

If you are interested in exploring the services of job specialists, begin by looking in the Yellow Pages of your telephone directory under these headings: Management Consultants, Employment, Resumes, Career Planning, and Social Services. Several career planning and employment services are available, ranging from highly generalized to very specific services. Most services claim they can help you. If you read this book, you will be in a better position to seek out specific services as well as ask the right questions for screening the services. You may even discover you know more about finding a job than many of the so-called professionals!

While many services are excellent,
other services are useless
and fraudulent.

ALTERNATIVE SERVICES

At least 10 different career planning and employment services are available to assist you with your job search. Each has certain advantages and disadvantages. Approach them with caution. Never sign a contract before you read the fine print, get a second opinion, and talk to former clients about the **results** they achieved through the service. With these words of caution in mind, let's take a look at the variety of services available.

1. Public employment services:

Public employment services usually consist of a state agency which provides employment assistance as well as dispenses unemployment compensation benefits. Employment assistance largely consists of job listings and counseling services. However, counseling services often are a front to screen individuals for employers who list with the public employment agency. If you want your career to regress by looking for entry-level jobs in the $10,000 to $16,000 range, contact this service. Most employers do not list with this service, especially for positions paying more than $18,000 a year. If you walk through one of these offices, you will find that most people are unemployed and look poor; they will likely remain so for some time. In fact, some experts believe we should abolish these offices altogether because they exacerbate unemployment; they take people away from the more productive channels for employment—personal contacts—and put them in a line to waste time and meet few helpful and positive people. Ex-educators should look elsewhere for assistance.

2. Private employment agencies:

Private employment agencies work for money, either from applicants or employers. Approximately 8,000 such agencies operate nationwide. Many are highly specialized in technical, scientific, and financial fields. The majority of these firms serve the interests of employers since employers—not applicants—represent repeat business. While employers normally pay the placement fee, many agencies charge applicants 10 to 15 percent of their first year salary. These firms have one major advantage: job leads which you may have difficulty uncovering elsewhere. Especially for highly specialized fields, a good firm can be extremely helpful. The major disadvantages are that they can be costly and the quality of the firms varies. Be careful in how you deal with them. Make sure you understand the fee structure and what they will do for you before you sign anything.

3. College/university placement offices:

College and university placement offices provide in-house career planning services for graduating students. While some give assistance to alumni, don't expect too much help if you already graduated. Many of these offices are understaffed or provide only rudimentary services, such as maintaining a career planning library, coordinating on-campus interviews for graduating seniors, and conducting workshops on how to write resumes and interview. Others provide a full range of well supported services including testing and one-on-one counseling. Indeed, many community colleges offer such services to members of the community on a walk-in basis. You can use their libraries and computerized career assessment programs, take personality and interest inventories, or attend special workshops or full-semester career planning courses which will take you through each step of the career planning and job search processes. You are well advised to enroll in such a course since it is likely to provide just enough structure and content to assess your motivated abilities and skills and to assist you in implementing a successful job search plan. Check with your local campus to see what services you might use.

4. Private career and job search firms:

Private career and job search firms help individuals acquire job search skills. They do not find you a job. In other words, they teach you much—maybe more but possibly less—of what is outlined in this book. Expect to pay anywhere from $1,500 to $10,000 for this service. If you need a structured environment for conducting your job search, contract with one of these firms. One of the most popular firms is Haldane Associates. Many of their pioneering career planning and job search methods are incorporated in this book. You will find branches of this nationwide firm in many major cities.

5. Executive search firms and headhunters:

Executive search firms work for employers in finding employees to fill critical positions in the $40,000 plus salary range.
They also are called *"headhunters"*, *"management consultants"*,
and *"executive recruiters"*. These firms play an important role
in linking high level technical and managerial talent to organizations. Don't expect to contract for these services. Executive
recruiters work for employers—not applicants. If a friend or
relative is in this business or you have relevant skills of interest
to these firms, let them know you are available — and ask for
their advice. On the other hand, you may want to contact firms
that specialize in recruiting individuals with your skill specialty.
Several books identify how you can best approach *"headhunters"* on your own: *How to Select and Use an Executive
Search Firm* (A. R. Taylor); *How to Answer a Headhunter's
Call* (Robert H. Perry); *The Headhunter Strategy* (Kenneth J.
Cole); *The Directory of Executive Recruiters* (Consultants
News); and *How to Get a Headhunter to Call* (Howard S.
Freedman).

6. Marketing services:

Marketing services represent an interesting combination of job
search and executive search activities. They can cost $2,500
or more, and they work with individuals anticipating a starting
salary of at least $40,000 but preferably over $60,000. These
firms try to minimize the time and risk of applying for jobs. A
typical operation begins with a client paying a $150 fee for
developing psychological, skills, and interests profiles. Next, a
marketing plan is outlined and a contract signed for specific
services. Using word processing equipment, the firm normally
develops a slick *"professional"* resume and mails it along with
a cover letter, to hundreds—maybe thousands—of firms. Clients
are then briefed and sent to interview with interested employers. While you can save money and achieve the same results
on your own, these firms do have one major advantage. They
save you *time* by doing most of the work for you. Again, approach these services with caution and with the knowledge that

you can probably do just as well—if not better—on your own by following the step-by-step advice of this and other jobs search books.

7. Women's Centers and special career services:

Women's Centers and special career services have been established to respond to the employment needs of special groups. Women's Centers are particularly active in sponsoring career planning workshops and job information networks. These centers tend to be geared toward elementary job search activities, because their clientele largely consists of housewives who are entering or re-entering the workforce with little knowledge of the job market. Special career services arise at times for different categories of employees. For example, unemployed aerospace engineers, teachers, veterans, air traffic controllers, and government employees have formed special groups for developing job search skills and sharing job leads.

8. Testing and assessment centers:

Testing and assessment centers provide assistance for identifying vocational skills, interests, and objectives. Usually staffed by trained professionals, these centers administer several types of tests and charge from $300 to $800 per person. You may wish to use some of these services if you feel our activities in Chapters Five, Six, and Seven generate insufficient information on your skills and interests to formulate your job objective. If you use such services, make sure you are given one or both of the two most popular and reliable tests: *Myers-Briggs Type Indicator* and the *Strong-Campbell Interest Inventory.* You should find both tests helpful in better understanding your interests and decision-making styles. However, try our exercises before you hire a psychologist or visit a testing center. If you first complete these exercises, you will be in a better position to know exactly what you need from such centers. In many cases the career office at your local community college or women's center can administer these tests at minimum cost.

9. Job fairs or career conferences:

Job fairs or career conferences are organized by employment agencies to link applicants to employers. Usually consisting of one to two-day meetings in a hotel, employers meet with applicants as a group and on a one-to-one basis. Employers give presentations on their companies, resumes are circulated, and candidates are interviewed. Many of these conferences are organized to attract hard-to-recruit groups, such as engineers, computer programmers, and clerical and service workers. These are excellent sources for job leads and information—if you get invited to the meeting or they are open to the public. Employers pay for this service—not applicants.

10. Professional associations:

Professional associations often provide placement assistance. This usually consists of listing job vacancies and organizing a job information exchange at annual conferences. These meetings are good sources for making job contacts in different geographic locations within a particular professional field. But don't expect too much. Talking to people (networking) at professional conferences will probably yield better results than reading job listings and interviewing at conference placement centers.

CHOOSE THE BEST

Other types of career planning and employment services are growing and specializing in particular occupational fields. You may wish to use these services as a supplement to this book.

Whatever you do, proceed with caution, know exactly what you are getting into, and choose the best. Remember, there is no such thing as a free lunch, and you often get less than what you pay for. At the same time, the most expensive services are not necessarily the best. Indeed, the free and inexpensive career planning services offered by many community colleges—libraries, computerized career assessment programs, testing, and workshops—are often much superior to the other alternative services which can be expensive. After reading this book, you should be able to make intelligent decisions about what, when, where, and with what results you can use professional assistance. Shop around, compare services and costs, ask questions, talk to former clients, and read the fine print with your lawyer before giving an employment expert a job using your hard earned money!

STRATEGIES FOR SUCCESS

Success is determined by more than just a good plan getting implemented. We know success is not determined primarily by intelligence, time management, or luck. Based upon experience, theory, research, common sense, and acceptance of some self-transformation principles, we believe you will achieve job search success by following many of the following 20 principles:

1. **You should work hard at finding a job:** Make this a daily endeavor and involve your family.

2. **You should not be discouraged with set-backs:** You are playing the odds, so expect disappointments and handle them in stride. You will get many *"no's"* before finding the one *"yes"* which is right for you.

3. **You should be patient and persevere:** Expect three months of hard work before you connect with the job that's right for you.

4. **You should be honest with yourself and others:** Honesty is always the best policy. But don't be naive and stupid by confessing your negatives and shortcomings to others.

5. **You should develop a positive attitude toward yourself:** Nobody wants to employ guilt-ridden people with inferiority complexes. Focus on your positive characteristics.

6. **You should associate with positive and successful people:** Finding a job largely depends on how well you relate to others. Avoid associating with negative and depressing people who complain and have a *"you-can't-do-it"* attitude. Run with winners who have a positive *"can-do"* outlook on life.

7. **You should set goals:** You should have a clear idea of what you want and where you are going. Without these, you will present a confusing and indecisive image to others. Clear goals help direct your job search into productive channels. Moreover, setting high goals will help make you work hard in getting what you want.

8. **You should plan:** Convert your goals into action steps that are organized as short, intermediate, and long-range plans.

9. **You should get organized:** Translate your plans into activities, targets, names, addresses, telephone numbers, and materials. Develop an efficient and effective filing system and use a large calendar for setting time targets and recording appointments and useful information.

10. **You should be a good communicator:** Take stock of your oral, written, and nonverbal communication skills. How well do you communicate? Since most aspects of your job search involve communicating with others, and communication skills are one of the most sought-after skills, always present yourself well both verbally and nonverbally.

11. **You should be energetic and enthusiastic:** Employers are attracted to positive people. They don't like negative and depressing people who toil at their work. Generate enthusiasm both verbally and nonverbally. Check on your telephone voice —it may be more unenthusiastic than your voice in face-to-face situations.

12. **You should ask questions:** Your best information comes from asking questions. Learn to develop intelligent questions that are non-aggressive, polite, and interesting to others. But don't ask too many questions.

13. **You should be a good listener:** Being a good listener is often more important than being a good questioner and talker. Learn to improve your face-to-face listening behavior (nonverbal cues) as well as remember and use information gained from others.

Make others feel they enjoyed talking with you, i.e., you are one of the few people who actually *listens* to what they say.

14. **You should be polite, courteous, and thoughtful:** Treat gate-keepers, especially receptionists and secretaries, like human beings. Avoid being aggressive or too assertive. Try to be polite, courteous, and gracious. Your social graces are being observed. Remember to send thank-you letters—a very thoughtful thing to do in a job search. Even if rejected, thank employers for the *"opportunity"* given to you. After all, they may later have addi-tional opportunities, and they will remember you.

15. **You should be tactful:** Watch what you say to others about other people and your background. Don't be a gossip, back-stabber, or confessor.

16. **You should maintain a professional stance:** Be neat in what you do and wear, and speak with the confidence, authority, and maturity of a professional.

17. **You should demonstrate your intelligence and competence:** Present yourself as someone who gets things done and achieves results—a *producer.* Employers generally seek people who are bright, hard working, responsible, communicate well, have positive personalities, maintain good interpersonal relations, are likeable, observe dress and social codes, take initiative, are talented, possess expertise in particular areas, use good judgment, are cooperative, trustworthy, and loyal, generate confidence and credibility, and are conventional. In other words, they like people who score in the *"excellent"* to *"outstanding"* categories of the annual performance evaluation.

18. **You should not overdo your job search:** Don't engage in overkill and bore everyone with your *"job search"* stories. Achieve balance in everything you do. Occasionally take a few days off to do nothing related to your job search. Develop a system of incentives and rewards—such as two non-job search days a week, if you accomplish targets A, B, C, and D.

19. **You should be open-minded and keep an eye open for "luck":** Too much planning can blind you to unexpected and fruitful opportunities. You should welcome serendipity. Learn to re-evaluate your goals and strategies. Seize new opportunities if they appear appropriate.

20. **You should evaluate your progress and adjust:** Take two hours once every two weeks and evaluate what you are doing and accomplishing. If necessary, tinker with your plans and reorganize your activities and priorities. Don't become too routinized and thereby kill creativity and innovation.

These principles should provide you with an initial orientation for starting your job search. As you become more experienced, you will develop your own set of operating principles that should work for you in particular employment situations.

Chapter Five

KNOW YOUR
SKILLS AND ABILITIES

We live in a skills-based society where individuals market their skills to employers in exchange for money, position, and power. The ease by which individuals change jobs and careers is directly related to their ability to communicate their skills to employers and then transfer their skills to new work settings. To best make the transition from education and position yourself in the job markets of today and tomorrow, you should pay particular attention to refining your present skills as well as acquiring new and more marketable skills.

IDENTIFY YOUR SKILLS

But before you can refine your skills or acquire additional skills, you need to know what skills you presently possess. Unfortunately, few people can identify and talk about their skills even though they possess hundreds of skills which they use on a regular basis. This becomes a real problem when they must write a resume or go to a job interview. Since employers want to know about your specific abilities and skills, you must learn to both identify and communicate your skills to employers. You should be able to explain what it is you do well and give examples relevant to employers' needs.

What skills do you already have to offer employers? As an educator, the first skills you think about may be those related to the subject matter you teach. The skills you wish to communicate to employers will be those things you already have demonstrated you can do in specific jobs. They are your demonstrated abilities to accomplish work specific tasks.

TYPES OF SKILLS

Most people possess two types of skills that define their accomplishments and strengths as well as enable them to enter and advance within the job market: work-content skills and functional skills. You need to acquaint yourself with these skills before communicating them to employers.

We assume you have already acquired certain **work-content skills** necessary to function effectively in today's job market. These *"hard skills"* are easy to recognize since they are often identified as *"qualifications"* for specific jobs; they are the subject of most educational and training programs. Work-content skills tend to be technical and job-specific in nature. Examples of such skills include proficiency in typing, programming computers, teaching history, or operating an X-ray machine. They may require formal training, are associated with specific trades or professions, are used only in certain job and career settings, and use a separate skills vocabulary, jargon, and subject matter for specifying technical qualifications for individuals entering and advancing in an occupation. While these skills do not transfer well from one occupation to another, they are critical for entering and advancing within certain occupations. They are skills you first demonstrated when you were hired as an educator.

At the same time, you possess numerous **functional/transferable skills** employers readily seek along with your work-content skills. These *"soft skills"* are associated with numerous job settings, are mainly acquired through experience rather than formal training, and can be communicated through a general vocabulary. Functional/transferable skills are less easy to recognize since they tend to be linked to **dealing with processes** (communicating, problem-solving, motivating) rather than **doing things** (programming a computer, building a house, teaching a subject). While most people have only a few work-content skills, they have numerous—perhaps as many as 300—functional/transferable skills. These skills enable job seekers to more easily change jobs. But you must first be aware of your functional skills before you can adequately relate them to the job market.

Most people view the world of work in traditional occupational job skill terms. This is a **structural view** of occupational realities. Occupational fields are seen as consisting of separate and distinct jobs which, in turn, require specific work-content skills. From this perspective, occupations and jobs are relatively self-contained entities. Social work, for example, is seen as being different from paralegal work; social workers, therefore, are not *"qualified"* to seek paralegal work.

Functional skills can be transferred from one job or career to another.

On the other hand, a **functional view** of occupations and jobs emphasizes similar characteristics among jobs as well as common linkages between different occupations. Although the structure of occupations and jobs may differ, they have similar functions. They involve working with people, data, processes, and objects. If you work with people, data, processes, and objects in one occupation, you can transfer that experience to other occupations which have similar functions. Once you understand how your skills relate to the functions as well as investigate the structure of different occupations, you should be prepared to make job changes from one occupational field to another. Whether you possess the necessary work-content skills to qualify for entry into the other occupational field is another question altogether.

The skills we identify and help you organize in this chapter are the functional skills career counselors normally emphasize when advising clients to assess their **strengths**. In contrast to work-content skills, functional skills can be transferred from one job or career to another. They enable educators to make some job and career changes without the need to acquire additional education and training. They constitute an important bridge for moving out of education.

Before you decide if you need more education or training, you should first assess both your functional and work-content skills to see how they can be transferred to other jobs and occupations. Once you do this, you should be better prepared to communicate your qualifications to employers with a rich skills-based vocabulary.

YOUR STRENGTHS

Regardless of what combination of work-content and functional skills you possess, a job search must begin with identifying your strengths. Without knowing these, your job search will lack content and focus. After all, your goal should be to find a job that is fit for you rather than one you think you might be able to fit into. Of course, you also want to find a job for which there is a demand. This particular focus requires a well-defined approach to identifying and communicating your skills to others. You can best do this by asking the right questions about your strengths and then conducting a systematic self-assessment of what you do best.

ASK THE RIGHT QUESTIONS

Knowing the right questions to ask will save you time and steer you into productive job search channels from the very beginning. Asking the wrong questions can cripple your job search efforts and leave you frustrated. The questions must be understood from the perspectives of both employers and applicants.

Two of the most humbling questions you will encounter in your job search are *"Why should I hire you?"* and *"What are your weaknesses?"* These questions are particularly important for educators who must be prepared to explain their nonteaching strengths to employers outside education. While employers may not directly ask these questions, they are asking them nonetheless. If you can't answer these questions in a positive manner—directly, indirectly, verbally, or nonverbally—your job search will likely founder and you will join the ranks of the unsuccessful and disillusioned job searchers who feel something is wrong with them. Individuals who have lost their jobs are particularly vulnerable to these questions since many have lowered self-esteem and self-image as a result of the job loss. Many such people focus on what is wrong rather than what is right about themselves. Such thinking creates self-fulfilling prophecies and is self-destructive in the job market. By all means avoid such negative thinking.

Employers want to hire your *value or strengths*—not your weaknesses. Since it is easier to identify and interpret weaknesses, employers look for indicators of your strengths by trying to identify your weaknesses. Your job is to communicate your strengths to employers. The more successful you are in doing this, the better off you will be in relation to both employers and fellow applicants.

Employers want to hire your
value or strengths—
not your weaknesses.

Unfortunately, many people work against their own best interests. Not knowing their strengths, they market their weaknesses by first identifying job vacancies and then trying to fit their *"qualifications"* into job descriptions. This approach often frustrates applicants; it presents a picture of a job market which is not interested in the applicant's strengths. This leads some people toward acquiring new skills which they hope will be marketable, even though they do not enjoy using them. Millions of individuals find themselves in such misplaced situations. Your task is to avoid joining the ranks of the misplaced and unhappy work force by first understanding your skills and then relating them to your interests and goals. In so doing, you will be in a better position to target your job search toward jobs that should become especially rewarding and fulfilling.

FUNCTIONAL/TRANSFERABLE SKILLS

We know most people stumble into jobs by accident. Some are at the right place at the right time to take advantage of a job or career opportunity. Others work hard at trying to fit into jobs listed in classified ads, employment agencies, and personnel offices; identified through friends and acquaintances; or found by knocking on doors. After 15 to 20 years in the work world, many people wish they had better planned their careers from the very start. All of a sudden they are unhappily locked into jobs because of retirement benefits and the family responsibilities of raising children and meeting monthly mortgage payments.

After 10 or 20 years of work experience, most people have a good idea of what they don't like to do. While their values are more set than when they first began working, many people are still unclear as to what they do well and how their skills fit into the job market. What other jobs, for example, might they be qualified to perform? If they have the opportunity to change jobs or careers—either voluntarily or forced through termination—and find the time to plan the change, they can move into jobs and careers which fit their skills.

The key to understanding your non-technical strengths is to identify your transferable or functional skills. Once you have done this, you will be better prepared to identify what it is you want to do. Moreover, your self-image and self-esteem will improve. Better still, you will be prepared to communicate your strengths to others through a rich skills-based vocabulary. These outcomes are critically important for writing your resume and letters as well as for conducting informational and job interviews.

Most functional/transferable skills can be classified into two general skills and trait categories—organizational/interpersonal skills and personality/work-style traits:

TYPES OF TRANSFERABLE SKILLS

Organizational and Interpersonal Skills

___ communicating	___ trouble shooting
___ problem solving	___ implementing
___ analyzing/assessing	___ self-understanding
___ planning	___ understanding
___ decision-making	___ setting goals
___ innovating	___ conceptualizing
___ thinking logically	___ generalizing
___ evaluating	___ managing time
___ identifying problems	___ creating
___ synthesizing	___ judging
___ forecasting	___ controlling
___ tolerating ambiguity	___ organizing
___ motivating	___ persuading
___ leading	___ encouraging
___ selling	___ improving
___ performing	___ designing
___ reviewing	___ consulting
___ attaining	___ teaching
___ team building	___ cultivating

___ updating   ___ advising
___ coaching   ___ training
___ supervising   ___ interpreting
___ estimating   ___ achieving
___ negotiating   ___ reporting
___ administering   ___ managing

Personality and Work-Style Traits

___ diligent   ___ honest
___ patient   ___ reliable
___ innovative   ___ perceptive
___ persistent   ___ assertive
___ tactful   ___ sensitive
___ loyal   ___ astute
___ successful   ___ risk taker
___ versatile   ___ easy going
___ enthusiastic   ___ calm
___ out-going   ___ flexible
___ expressive   ___ competent
___ adaptable   ___ punctual
___ democratic   ___ receptive
___ resourceful   ___ diplomatic
___ determining   ___ self-confident
___ creative   ___ tenacious
___ open   ___ discrete
___ objective   ___ talented
___ warm   ___ empathic
___ orderly   ___ tidy
___ tolerant   ___ candid
___ frank   ___ adventuresome
___ cooperative   ___ firm
___ dynamic   ___ sincere
___ self-starter   ___ initiator
___ precise   ___ competent
___ sophisticated   ___ diplomatic
___ effective   ___ efficient

Let's specify the concept of functional/transferable skills for educators. Many educators view their skills in strict work-content terms—knowledge of a particular subject matter such as math, history, English, physics, or music. When looking outside education for employment, many seek jobs which will use their subject matter skills. However, they soon discover that non-educational institutions are not a ready market for such *"skills"*.

On the other hand, educators possess many other skills that are directly transferable to business and industry. Unaware of these skills, many educators fail to communicate their strengths to others. For example, research shows that graduate students in the humanities most frequently possess these transferable skills, in order of importance:

___ critical thinking	___ general knowledge
___ research techniques	___ cultural perspective
___ perseverance	___ teaching ability
___ self-discipline	___ self-confidence
___ insight	___ imagination
___ writing	___ leadership ability

A high degree of congruency exists between the most important skills individuals acquired in graduate school and those used to their present jobs outside education. Not surprisingly, leadership ability is one of the weakest skills acquired in graduate school. This is probably true of graduates in other disciplines. After all, graduate students are followers of mentors; they have few opportunities to acquire leadership roles and skills.

The fact that leadership ability and self-confidence rank low on the transferable skills totem-pole does not speak well for graduate training.

Most graduate students know that success in graduate school does not depend on exceptional intelligence. Successful graduate students have two critical skills and qualities: *analytical thinking and perseverance.* Analytical thinking—the ability to organize large amounts of data into new and coherent schemes, as well as the ability to think critically, use imagination, and gain insights—is one of the the most sought-after judgment job skills outside education. Other highly valued transferable skills are perseverance and self-discipline. The fact that leadership ability and self-confidence rank low on the transferable skills totem-pole does not speak well for graduate training in the humanities nor does such training appear to assist graduates in seeking responsible management positions outside education. This finding also points to one problem some readers may need to address in conducting their job search campaign: develop greater self-confidence, self-esteem, and leadership abilities.

Educators possess many of these graduate school skills as well as many additional transferable skills acquired while performing the role of educator. *Teaching*, for example, involves several skills other than instructing:

___ organizing	___ problem solving	___ coordinating
___ making decisions	___ public speaking	___ managing
___ counseling	___ advising	___ reporting
___ motivating	___ coaching	___ administering
___ leading	___ evaluating	___ persuading
___ selling	___ training	___ encouraging
___ assessing	___ supervising	___ improving

Research and publication activities involve many additional transferable skills:

___ initiating	___ interpreting	___ analyzing
___ updating	___ planning	___ designing
___ communicating	___ estimating	___ implementing
___ performing	___ achieving	___ reviewing
___ attaining	___ negotiating	___ maintaining responsibility

Interacting with students, faculty, administrators, staff, and the community requires using several skill-related personality qualities:

___ dynamic	___ unique	___ challenging
___ imaginative	___ versatile	___ sophisticated
___ innovative	___ responsible	___ diplomatic
___ perceptive	___ concerned	___ discrete

___ outstanding	___ successful	___ creative
___ tactful	___ easy-going	___ effective
___ reliable	___ humanistic	___ adept
___ vigorous	___ competent	___ efficient
___ sensitive	___ objective	___ honest
___ accurate	___ warm	___ aware
___ trained	___ broad	___ self-starter
___ expert	___ outgoing	___ strong
___ astute	___ experienced	___ talented
___ calm	___ democratic	___ empathic

Educators use numerous skills which go beyond simply teaching and conducting research in highly specialized and esoteric subjects. While many educators are unaware of the multiplicity and variety of their transferable skills, employers outside education are similarly uninformed. Consequently, educators must first educate themselves concerning their 500 to 800 transferable skills, and then communicate their skills to employers outside education. Thus, the skills identification approach enhances the important communication function between job seekers and employers.

Use the following exercises to identify both your work-content and transferable skills. These self-assessment techniques stress your positives or strengths rather than identify your negatives or weaknesses. They should generate a rich vocabulary for communicating your *"qualifications"* to employers. Each exercise requires different investments of your time and effort as well as varying degrees of assistance from other people.

If you feel these exercises are inadequate for your needs, by all means seek professional assistance from a testing or assessment center staffed by a licensed psychologist. These centers do in-depth testing which goes further than these self-directed skill exercises.

CHECKLIST METHOD

This is the simplest method for identifying your strengths. Review the different types of transferable skills outlined on pages 88-92. Place a "1" in front of the skills that *strongly* characterize you; assign a "2" to those skills that describe you to a *large extent*; put a "3" before those that describe you to *some extent*. After completing this exercise, review the lists and rank order the 10 characteristics that best describe you on each list.

SKILLS MAP

Richard N. Bolles has produced two well-known exercises for identifying transferable skills based upon John Holland's typology of work environments. In his book, *The Three Boxes of Life* (Ten Speed Press), he develops a checklist of 100 transferable skills. They are organized into 12 categories or types of skills: using hands, body, words, senses, numbers, intuition, analytical thinking, creativity, helpfulness, artistic abilities, leadership, and follow-through.

Bolles' second exercise, *"The Quick Job Hunting Map"*, expands upon this first one. The *"Map"* is a checklist of 222 skills. This exercise requires you to identify seven of your most satisfying accomplishments, achievements, jobs, or roles. After writing a page about each experience, you relate each to the checklist of 222 skills. The *"Map"* should give you a comprehensive picture of what skills you (1) use most frequently, and (2) enjoy using in satisfying and successful settings. While this exercise may take six hours to complete, it yields an enormous amount of data on past strengths. Furthermore, the *"Map"* generates a rich skills vocabulary for communicating your strengths to others. The *"Map"* is found in the appendix of Bolles' *What Color Is Your Parachute?* (Ten Speed Press) or it can be purchased separately in beginning, advanced, or new versions from Ten Speed Press. His books as well as the latest version (1990) of his popular *New Quick Job Hunting Map* can be ordered directly from Impact Publications by completing the order information as the end of this book.

AUTOBIOGRAPHY OF ACCOMPLISHMENTS

Write a lengthy essay about your life accomplishments. This could range from 20 to 100 pages. After completing the essay, go through it page by page to identify what you most enjoyed doing (working with different kinds of information, people, and things) and what skills you used most frequently as well as enjoyed using. Finally, identify those skills you wish to continue using. After analyzing and synthesizing this data, you should have a relatively clear picture of your strongest skills.

COMPUTERIZED SKILLS ASSESSMENT SYSTEMS

While the previous self-directed exercises required you to either respond to checklists of skills or reconstruct and analyze your past job experiences, several computerized self-assessment programs are designed to help individuals identify their skills. Many of the programs are available in schools, colleges, and libraries. Some of the most widely used programs include:

- *Discover II*
- *Sigi-Plus*
- *Computerized Career Assessment and Planning Program*

These comprehensive career planning programs do much more than assess skills. As we will see in Chapter Seven, they also integrate other key components in the career planning process—interests, goals, related jobs, college majors, education and training programs, and job search plans. These programs are widely available in schools, colleges, and libraries across the country. You might check with the career or counseling center at your local community college to see what computerized career assessment systems are available for your use. They are relatively easy to use and they generate a great deal of useful career planning information.

Chapter Six

SPECIFY YOUR INTERESTS AND VALUES

Knowing what you do well is essential to understanding your strengths and for linking your capabilities to jobs outside education. However, just knowing your abilities and skills will not give your job search the direction it needs for finding jobs outside education. You also need to know your work values and interests. These are the basic building blocks for setting goals and targeting your abilities toward certain jobs and careers.

Take, for example, the individual who types 120 words a minute. While this person possesses a highly marketable skill, if the person doesn't enjoy using this skill and is more interested in working outdoors, this will not become a motivated skill; the individual will most likely not pursue a typing job. Your interests and values will determine whether or not certain skills should play a central role in your job search.

VOCATIONAL INTERESTS

We all have interests. Most change over time. Ten years ago, for example, you may have been interested in organizing academic courses, promoting student activities, or pursuing an advanced degree. Today, many of your interests may lie elsewhere.

Many of your interests may center on your present job whereas others relate to activities that define your hobbies and leisure activities. A good place to start identifying your interests is by examining the information and exercises found in the *Guide to Occupational Exploration*. Widely used by students and others first entering the job market, it is also relevant to educators and others who already have work experience. The guide classifies all jobs in the United States into 12 interest areas. Examine the following list of interest areas. In the first column check those work areas that appeal to you. In the second column rank order those areas you checked in the first column. Start with "1" to indicate the most interesting:

YOUR WORK INTERESTS

Yes/No (x)	Ranking (1-12)	Interest Area
____	____	**Artistic:** an interest in creative expression of feelings or ideas.
____	____	**Scientific:** an interest in discovering, collecting, and analyzing information about the natural world, and in applying scientific research findings to problems in medicine, the life sciences, and the nature sciences.
____	____	**Plants and animals:** an interest in working with plants and animals, usually outdoors.
____	____	**Protective:** an interest in using authority to protect people and property.
____	____	**Mechanical:** an interest in applying mechanical principles to practical situations by using machines or hand tools.
____	____	**Industrial:** an interest in repetitive, concrete, organized activities done in a factory setting.

_____   _____   **Business detail:** an interest in organized, clearly defined activities requiring accuracy and attention to details, primarily in an office setting.

_____   _____   **Selling:** an interest in bringing others to a particular point of view by personal persuasion, using sales and promotion techniques.

_____   _____   **Accommodating:** an interest in catering to the wishes and needs of others, usually on a one-to-one basis.

_____   _____   **Humanitarian:** an interest in helping others with their mental, spiritual, social, physical, or vocational needs.

_____   _____   **Leading and influencing:** an interest in leading and influencing others by using high-level verbal or numerical abilities.

_____   _____   **Physical performing:** an interest in physical activities performed before an audience.

The *Guide for Occupational Exploration* also includes other checklists relating to home-based and leisure activities that may or may not relate to your work interests. If you are unclear about your work interests, you might want to consult these other interest exercises. You may discover that some of your home-based and leisure activity interests should become your work interests. Examples of such interests include:

LEISURE AND HOME-BASED INTERESTS

_____   Acting in a play or amateur variety show.

_____   Advising family members on their personal problems.

_____   Announcing or emceeing a program.

____ Applying first aid in emergencies as a volunteer.

____ Building model airplanes, automobiles, or boats.

____ Building or repairing radio or television sets.

____ Buying large quantities of food or other products for an organization.

____ Campaigning for political candidates or issues.

____ Canning and preserving food.

____ Carving small wooden objects.

____ Coaching children or youth in sports activities.

____ Collecting experiments involving plants.

____ Conducting house-to-house or telephone surveys for a PTA or other organization.

____ Creating or styling hairdos for friends.

____ Designing your own greeting cards and writing original verses.

____ Developing film.

____ Doing impersonations.

____ Doing public speaking or debating.

____ Entertaining at parties or other events.

____ Helping conduct physical exercises for disabled people.

____ Making ceramic objects.

____ Modeling clothes for a fashion show.

____ Mounting and framing pictures.

____ Nursing sick pets.

____ Painting the interior or exterior of a home.

____ Playing a musical instrument.

____ Refinishing or re-upholstering furniture.

____ Repairing electrical household appliances.

____ Repairing the family car.

____ Repairing or assembling bicycles.

____ Repairing plumbing in the house.

____   Speaking on radio or television.

____   Taking photographs.

____   Teaching in Sunday School.

____   Tutoring pupils in school subjects.

____   Weaving rugs or making quilts.

____   Writing articles, stories, or plays.

____   Writing songs for club socials or amateur plays.

Indeed, many people turn hobbies or home activities into full-time jobs after deciding that such *"work"* is what they really enjoy doing.

Other popular exercises designed to identify your work interests include John Holland's *"The Self-Directed Search"* which is found in his book, **Making Vocational Choices: A Theory of Careers**. It is also published as a separate testing instrument, **The Self-Directed Search—A Guide to Educational and Vocational Planning**. Developed from Holland's Vocational Preference Inventory, this popular self-administered, self-scored, and self-interpreted inventory helps individuals quickly identify what type of work environment they are motivated to seek—realistic, investigative, artistic, social, enterprising, or conventional—and aligns these work environments with lists of common occupational titles. An easy exercise to use, it gives you a quick overview of your orientation toward different types of work settings that interest you.

Holland's self-directed search is also the basic framework used in developing Bolles' *"The Quick Job Hunting Map"* as found in his **What Color Is Your Parachute?** and **The New Quick Job Hunting Map** books.

For more sophisticated treatments of work interests, which are also validated through testing procedures, contact a career counselor, women's center, or testing and assessment center for information on the following tests:

- Strong-Campbell Interest Inventory
- Myers-Briggs Type Indicator
- Edwards Personal Preference Schedule
- Kuder Occupational Interest Survey
- APTICOM
- Jackson Vocational Interest Survey

- Ramak Inventory
- Vocational Interest Inventory
- Career Assessment Inventory
- Temperament and Values Inventory

Numerous other job and career interest inventories are also available. For further information, contact a career counselor or consult Educational Testing Service which compiles such tests. *The ETS Test Collection Catalog* (New York: Oryx Press), which is available in many library reference sections, lists most of these tests. The *Mental Measurements Yearbook* (Lincoln, NE: University of Nebraska Press) also surveys many of the major testing and assessment instruments.

Not all testing and assessment instruments used by career counselors are equally valid for career planning purposes.

Keep in mind that not all testing and assessment instruments used by career counselors are equally valid for career planning purposes. While the Strong-Campbell Interest Inventory appears to be the most relevant for career decision-making, the Myers-Briggs Type Indicator has become extremely popular during the past two years. It is more useful for measuring individual personality and decision-making styles than for predicting career choices. It is most widely used in pastoral counseling, student personnel, and business and religious organizations for measuring personality and decision-making styles. How these elements relate to career choices remains uncertain. In the meantime, many career counselors find Holland's *The Self-Directed Search* an excellent self-directed alternative to these professionally administered and interpreted tests.

WORK VALUES

Work values are those things you like to do. They give you pleasure and enjoyment. Most jobs involve a combination of likes and dislikes. By identifying what you both like and dislike about jobs, you should be able to better identify jobs that involve tasks that you will most enjoy.

Several exercises can help you identify your work values. First, identify what most satisfies you about work by completing the following exercise:

MY WORK VALUES

I prefer employment which enables me to:

_____	contribute to society	_____	be creative
_____	have contact with people	_____	supervise others
_____	work alone	_____	work with details
_____	work with a team	_____	gain recognition
_____	compete with others	_____	acquire security
_____	make decisions	_____	make a lot of money
_____	work under pressure	_____	help others
_____	use power and authority	_____	solve problems
_____	acquire new knowledge	_____	take risks
_____	be a recognized expert	_____	work at my own pace

Select four work values from the above list which are the most important to you and list them in the space below. List any other work values (desired satisfactions) which were not listed above but are nonetheless important to you:

1. _____

2. _____

3. _____

4. _____

_____

_____

Another approach to identifying work values is outlined in the **Guide to Occupational Exploration.** If you feel you need to go beyond the above exercises, try this one. In the first column check those values that are most important to you. In the second column rank order the five most important values:

RANKING WORK VALUES

Yes/No (x)	Ranking (1-5)	Work Values
_____	_____	**Adventure:** Working in a job that requires taking risks.
_____	_____	**Authority:** Working in a job in which you use your position to control others.
_____	_____	**Competition:** Working in a job in which you compete with others.
_____	_____	**Creativity and self-expression:** Working in a job in which you use your imagination to find new ways to do or say something.
_____	_____	**Flexible work schedule:** Working in a job in which you choose your hours to work.
_____	_____	**Helping others:** Working in a job in which you provide direct services to persons with problems.
_____	_____	**High salary:** Working in a job where many workers earn a large amount of money.
_____	_____	**Independence:** Working in a job in which you decide for yourself what work to do and how to do it.

_____   _____   **Influencing others:** Working in a job in which you influence the opinions of others or decisions of others.

_____   _____   **Intellectual stimulation:** Working in a job which requires a great amount of thought and reasoning.

_____   _____   **Leadership:** Working in a job in which you direct, manage, or supervise the activities of others.

_____   _____   **Outside work:** Working out-of-doors.

_____   _____   **Persuading:** Working in a job which you personally convince others to take certain actions.

_____   _____   **Physical work:** Working in a job in which requires substantial physical activity.

_____   _____   **Prestige:** Working in a job which gives you status and respect in the community.

_____   _____   **Public attention:** Working in a job in which you attract immediate notice because of appearance or activity.

_____   _____   **Public contact:** Working in a job in which you have day-to-day dealings with the public.

_____   _____   **Recognition:** Working in a job in which you gain public notice.

_____   _____   **Research work:** Working in a job in which you search for and discover new facts and develop ways to apply them.

_____   _____   **Routine work:** Working in a job in which you follow established procedures requiring little change.

_____   _____   **Seasonal work:** Working in a job in which you are employed only at certain times of the year.

_____   _____   **Travel:** Working in a job in which you take frequent trips.

_____   _____   **Variety:** Working in a job in which your duties change frequently.

_____   _____   **Work with children:** Working in a job in which you teach or otherwise care for children.

_____   _____   **Work with hands:** Working in a job in which you use your hands or hand tools.

_____   _____   **Work with machines or equipment:** Working in a job in which you use machines or equipment.

_____   _____   **Work with numbers:** Working in a job in which you use mathematics or statistics.

Second, develop a comprehensive list of your past and present *job frustrations and dissatisfactions.* This should help you identify negative factors you should avoid in future jobs.

MY JOB FRUSTRATIONS
AND DISSATISFACTIONS

List as well as rank order as many past and present things that
frustrate or make you dissatisfied and unhappy in job situations:

Rank

1. _____   _____

2. _____   _____

3. _____   _____

4. _____   _____

5. _____   _____

6. _____   _____

7. _____   _____

8. _____   _____

9. _____   _____

10. _____   _____

Third, brainstorm a list of *"Ten or More Things I Love to Do"*. Identify
which ones could be incorporated into what kinds of work environments:

TEN OR MORE THINGS I LOVE TO DO

	Item	Related Work Environment
1.	_____	_____
2.	_____	_____
3.	_____	_____
4.	_____	_____
5.	_____	_____

6. _____   _____
7. _____   _____
8. _____   _____
9. _____   _____
10. _____   _____

Fourth, list at least ten things you most enjoy about work and rank each item accordingly:

TEN THINGS I ENJOY THE MOST ABOUT WORK

Rank

1. _____ _____
2. _____ _____
3. _____ _____
4. _____ _____
5. _____ _____
6. _____ _____
7. _____ _____
8. _____ _____
9. _____ _____
10. _____ _____

Fifth, you should also identify the types of interpersonal environments you prefer working in. Do this by specifying the types of people you like and dislike associating with:

```
┌─────────────── INTERPERSONAL ENVIRONMENTS ───────────────┐
│                                                          │
│     Characteristics of people        Characteristics of people │
│        I like working with:            I dislike working with: │
│                                                          │
│     _____        _____ │
│                                                          │
│     _____        _____ │
│                                                          │
│     _____        _____ │
│                                                          │
│     _____        _____ │
│                                                          │
│     _____        _____ │
│                                                          │
│     _____        _____ │
│                                                          │
│     _____        _____ │
│                                                          │
│     _____        _____ │
│                                                          │
│     _____        _____ │
│                                                          │
└──────────────────────────────────────────────────────────┘
```

COMPUTERIZED SYSTEMS

Several computerized self-assessment programs are available that largely focus on career interests and values. The two major systems outlined in Chapter Five for identifying abilities and skills—*Discover II* and *Sigi-Plus*—also include career interest segments. Some other popular systems are:

- *Career Interest Program*
- *Computerized Career Assessment and Planning Program*
- *Computerized Career Information System*
- *Values Auction Deluxe*

You should be able to get access to some of these and other related computer programs through your local community college, career center, or library.

YOUR FUTURE AS OBJECTIVES

All of these exercises are designed to explore your past and present work-related values. At the same time, you need to project your values into the *future*. What, for example, do you want to do over the next 10 to 20 years? We'll return to this type of value question when we address the critical objective setting stage of the job search process in Chapter Eight.

Chapter Seven

KNOW YOUR MOTIVATED ABILITIES AND SKILLS (MAS)

Once you know what you do well and enjoy doing, you next need to analyze those interests, values, abilities, and skills that form a *recurring motivated pattern*. This pattern is the single most important piece of information you need to know about yourself in the whole self-assessment process. Knowing your skills and abilities alone without knowing how they relate to your interests and values will not give your job search the direction it needs for finding the right job outside education.

WHAT'S YOUR MAS?

The concept of motivated abilities and skills (MAS) enables us to relate your interests and values to your skills and abilities. But how do we identify your MAS beyond the questions and exercises outlined thus far?

Your pattern of motivated abilities and skills becomes evident once you analyze your *achievements or accomplishments*. For it is your achievements that tell us what you both did well and enjoyed doing. If we analyze and synthesize many of your achievements, we are likely to identify a *recurring pattern* that most likely goes back to your childhood and which will continue to characterize your achievements in the future.

Numerous self-directed exercises can assist you in identifying your pattern of motivated abilities and skills. The basic requirements for making these exercises work for you are time and analytical ability. You must spend a great deal of time detailing your achievements by looking at your past history of accomplishments. Once you complete the historical reconstruction task, you must comb through your *"stories"* to identify recurring themes and patterns. This requires a high level of analytical ability which you may or may not possess. If analysis and synthesis are not two of your strong skills, you may need to seek assistance from a friend or professional who is good at analyzing and synthesizing information presented in narrative form. Career counseling firms such as Haldane Associates and People Management, Inc. are known for their use of this type of motivated pattern approach; they should be able to assist you.

Several paper and pencil exercises are designed to help identify your pattern of motivated abilities and skills. We outline some of the most popular and thorough such exercises that have proved useful to thousands of people.

THE SKILLS MAP

Richard Bolles' *"Quick Job Hunting Map"* has become a standard self-assessment tool for thousands of job seekers and career changers who are willing to spend the time and effort necessary for discovering their pattern of motivated abilities and skills. Offering a checklist of over 200 skills organized around John Holland's concept of *"The Self-Directed Search"* for defining work environments (realistic, investigative, artistic, social, enterprising, and conventional), the *"Map"* requires you to identify seven of your most satisfying accomplishments, achievements, jobs, or roles. After detailing each achievement, you analyze the details of each in relation to the checklist of skills. Once you do this for all seven achievements, you should generate a comprehensive picture of what skills you (1) use most frequently, and (2) enjoy using in satisfying and successful settings. This exercise not only yields an enormous amount of information on your interests, values, skills, and abilities, it also assists you in the process of analyzing the data. If done property, the *"Map"* should also generate a rich *"skills"* vocabulary which you should use in your resumes and letters as well as in interviews.

The *"Map"* is available in different forms and for different levels of experience. The most popular versions are found in the Appendix of Bolles' **What Color Is Your Parachute?** and **The Three Boxes of Life** as well as in a separate publication entitled *The New Quick Job Hunting Map*. These three publications can be ordered directly from Impact Publications by completing the order information at the end of this book. The map is also available in three other versions: *The Beginning Quick Job-Hunting Map, How to Create a Picture of Your Ideal Job or Next Career*, and *The Classic Quick Job-Hunting Map*. These versions of the *"Map"* are most conveniently available directly from the publisher, Ten Speed Press (P.O. Box 7123, Berkeley, CA 94707).

We highly recommend using the Map because of the ease in which it can be used. If you will spend the six to 20 hours necessary to complete it properly, the *"Map"* will give you some important information about yourself. Unfortunately, many people become overwhelmed by the exercise and either decide not to complete it or they try to save time by not doing it according to the directions. You simply must follow the directions and spend the time and effort necessary if you want to get the maximum benefit from this exercise.

Keep in mind that like most self-assessment devices, there is nothing magical about the *"Map"*. Its basic organizing principles are simple. Like other exercises designed to uncover your pattern of motivated abilities and skills, this one is based on a theory of historical determinism and probability. In other words, once you uncover your pattern, get prepared to acknowledge it and live with it in the future.

Once you uncover your pattern, get prepared to acknowledge it and live with it in the future.

AUTOBIOGRAPHY OF ACCOMPLISHMENTS

Less structured than the *"Map"* device, this exercise requires you to write a lengthy essay about your life accomplishments. Your essay may run anywhere from 20 to 200 pages. After completing it, go through it page by page to identify what you most enjoyed doing (working with different kinds of data, people, processes, and objects) and what skills you used most frequently as well as enjoyed using. Finally, identify those skills you wish to continue using. After analyzing and synthesizing this data, you should have a relatively clear picture of your strongest skills.

This exercise requires a great deal of self-discipline and analytic skill. To do it properly, you must write as much as possible, and in as much detail as possible, about your accomplishments. The richer the detail, the better will be your analysis.

MOTIVATED SKILLS EXERCISE

Our final exercise is one of the most complex and time consuming self-assessment exercises. However, it yields some of the best data on motivated abilities and skills, and it is especially useful for those who feel they need a more thorough analysis of their past achievements. This device is widely used by career counselors. Initially developed by Haldane Associates, this particular exercise is variously referred to as *"Success Factor Analysis"*, *"System to Identify Motivated Skills"*, or *"Intensive Skills Identification"*.

This technique helps you identify which skills you *enjoy* using. While you can use this technique on your own, it is best to work with someone else. Since you will need six to eight hours to properly complete this exercise, divide your time into two or three work sessions.

The exercise consists of six steps. The steps follow the basic pattern of generating raw data, identifying patterns, analyzing the data through reduction techniques, and synthesizing the patterns into a transferable skills vocabulary. You need strong analytical skills to complete this exercise on your own. The six steps include:

1. **Identify 15-20 achievements:** These consist of things you enjoyed doing, believe you did well, and felt a sense of satisfaction, pride, or accomplishment in doing. You can see yourself performing at your best and enjoying your experiences when you analyze your achievements. This information reveals your motivations since it deals entirely with your voluntary behavior. In addition, it identifies what is right with you by focusing on your positives and strengths. Identify achievements throughout your life, beginning with your childhood. Your achievements should relate to specific experiences—not general ones—and may be drawn from work, leisure, education, military,

or home life. Put each achievement at the top of a separate sheet of paper. For example, your achievements might appear as follows:

SAMPLE ACHIEVEMENT STATEMENTS

"When I was 10 years old, I started a small paper route and built it up to the largest in my district."

"I started playing chess in ninth grade and earned the right to play first board on my high school chess team in my junior year."

"Learned to play the piano and often played for church services while in high school."

"Designed and constructed a dress for a 4-H demonstration project."

"Although I was small compared to other guys, I made the first string on my high school football team."

"I graduated from high school with honors even though I was very active in school clubs and had to work part-time."

"I was the first in my family to go to college and one of the few from my high school. Worked part-time and summers. A real struggle, but I made it."

"Earned an 'A' grade on my senior psychology project from a real tough professor."

"Finished my master's degree while teaching full-time and attending to my family responsibilities."

"Got an 'A' in student teaching."

"Proposed a chef's course for junior high boys. Got it approved. Developed it into a very popular elective."

"Developed a career education project for my students which involved their parents and some local businesses. Had media coverage and lots of recognition."

"Wrote and finished my dissertation."

"Designed the plans for our house and had it constructed within budget."

"Have developed a reputation as a good teacher. I especially enjoy working with the so-called apathetic students and getting them involved and interests in the subject matter."

"Designed three new courses for my department and had them approved."

"Chaired a special committee which investigated the school's recruiting and selection procedures and wrote the final report."

2. Prioritize your seven most significant achievements.

YOUR MOST SIGNIFICANT ACHIEVEMENTS

1. _____
2. _____
3. _____
4. _____
5. _____
6. _____
7. _____

3. **Write a full page on each of your prioritized achievements.** You should describe:

   • How you initially became involved.
   • The details of **what you did** and **how you did it**.
   • What was especially enjoyable or satisfying to you.

   Use copies of the following form to outline your achievements.

DETAILING YOUR ACHIEVEMENTS

ACHIEVEMENT # ___ : _____

_____

1. **How did I initially become involved?** _____

   _____

   _____

2. **What did I do?** _____

   _____

   _____

   _____

_____

_____

3. **How did I do it?** _____

_____

_____

_____

_____

4. **What was especially enjoyable about doing it?**

_____

_____

_____

4. **Elaborate on your achievements:** Have one or two other people interview you. For each achievement have them note on a separate sheet of paper any terms used to reveal your skills, abilities, and personal qualities. To elaborate details, the interviewer(s) may ask:

    - *What was involved in the achievement?*
    - *What was your part?*
    - *What did you actually do?*
    - *How did you go about that?*

    Clarify any vague areas by providing an example or illustration of what you actually did. Probe with the following questions:

    - *Would you elaborate on one example of what you mean?*
    - *Could you give me an illustration?*
    - *What were you good at doing?*

    This interview should clarify the details of your activities by asking only *"what"* and *"how"* questions. It should take 45 to 90 minutes to complete. Reproduce the following *"Strength Iden-tification Interview"* form to guide you through this interview.

STRENGTH IDENTIFICATION INTERVIEW

Interviewee _____   **Interviewer** _____

INSTRUCTIONS: For each achievement experience, identify the *skills* and abilities the achiever actually demonstrates. Obtain details of the experience by asking *what* was involved with the achievement and *how* the individual made the achievement happen. Avoid *"why"* questions which tend to mislead. Ask for examples or illustrations of what and how.

Achievement # ___   **Achievement #** ___   **Achievement #** ___

Recurring abilities and skills:

5. **Identify patterns by examining the interviewer's notes:** Together identify the recurring skills, abilities, and personal qualities **demonstrated** in your achievements. Search for patterns. Your skills pattern should be clear at this point; you should feel comfortable with it. If you have questions, review the data. If you disagree with a conclusion, disregard it. The results must accurately and honestly reflect how you operate.

6. **Synthesize the information by clustering similar skills into categories:** For example, your skills might be grouped in the following manner:

SYNTHESIZED SKILL CLUSTERS

Investigate/Survey/Read Inquire/Probe/Question	Teach/Train/Drill Perform/Show/Demonstrate
Learn/Memorize/Practice Evaluate/Appraise/Assess/ Compare	Construct/Assemble/Put together
	Organize/Structure/Provide definition/Plan/Chart course Strategize/Coordinate
Influence/Involve/Get participation/Publicize Promote	Create/Design/Adapt/Modify

This exercise yields a relatively comprehensive inventory of your skills. The information will better enable you to use a **skills vocabulary** when identifying your objective, writing your resume and letters, and interviewing. Your self-confidence and self-esteem should increase accordingly.

OTHER ALTERNATIVES

Several other techniques also can help you identify your motivated abilities and skills:

1. List all of your hobbies and analyze what you do in each, which ones you like the most, what skills you use, and your accomplishments.

2. Conduct a job analysis by writing about your past jobs and identifying which skills you used in each job. Cluster the skills into related categories and prioritize them according to your preferences.

3. Purchase of copy of Arthur F. Miller and Ralph T. Mattson's *The Truth About You* and work through the exercises found in the Appendix. This is an abbreviated version of the authors' SIMA (System for Identifying Motivated Abilities) technique used by their career counseling firm, People Management, Inc. (10 Station Street, Simsbury, CT 06070). If you need professional assistance, contact this firm directly. They can provide you with several alternative services consistent with the career planning philosophy and approach outlined in this chapter.

4. Complete John Holland's *"The Self-Directed Search"*. You'll find it in his book, *Making Vocational Choices: A Theory of Careers* or in a separate publication entitled *The Self-Directed Search—A Guide to Educational and Vocational Planning.*

BENEFIT FROM REDUNDANCY

The self-directed MAS exercises generate similar information. They identify interests, values, abilities, and skills you already possess. While aptitude and achievement tests may yield similar information, the self-directed exercises have three major advantages over the standardized tests: less expensive, self-monitored and evaluated, and measure motivation *and* ability.

Completing each exercise demands a different investment of your time. Writing your life history and completing the Motivated Skills Exercise as well as Bolles' *"Map"* are the most time consuming. On the other hand, Holland's *"Self-Directed Search"* can be completed in a few minutes. But the more time you invest with each technique, the more useful information you will generate. We recommend creating redundancy by using at least two or three different techniques. This will help reinforce and confirm the validity of your observations and interpretations. If you have a great deal of work experience, we recommend using the more thorough exercises. The more you put into these techniques and exercises, the greater the benefit to other stages of your job search. You will be well prepared to target your job search toward specific jobs that fit your MAS as well as communicate your qualifications loud and clear to employers outside education. A carefully planned career change should not do less than this.

Past performance is the best predictor of future performance.

BRIDGING YOUR PAST AND FUTURE

Many people want to know about their futures. If you expect the self-assessment techniques in Chapters Five, Six, and Seven to spell out your future, you will be disappointed. Fortune tellers, horoscopes, and various forms of mysticism may be what you need.

These are historical devices which integrate past achievements, abilities, and motivations for projecting future performance. They clarify past strengths and recurring motivations for targeting future jobs. Abilities and motivations are the *qualifications* employers expect for particular jobs. Qualifications consist of your past experience *and* your motivated abilities and skills.

The assessment techniques provide a bridge between your past and future. As such, they treat your future preferences and performance as functions of your past experiences and demonstrated abilities. This common sense notion is shared among employers: past performance is the best predictor of future performance.

Yet, employers hire a person's *future* rather than their past. And herein lies an important problem you can help employers overcome. Getting the job that is right for you entails communicating to prospective employers that you have the necessary qualifications. Indeed, employers will look for signs of your future productivity *for them*. You are an unknown and risky quality. Therefore, you must communicate evidence of your past productivity. This evidence is revealed clearly in your past achievements which you outlined by using these assessment techniques.

The overall value of using these assessment techniques is that they should enhance your occupational mobility over the long-run. The major thrust of all these techniques is to identify abilities and skills which are *transferable* to different work environments. This is particularly important to educators who are looking for career alternatives outside education but who tend to think about their abilities, skills, and qualifications in traditional terms. Employers may view you initially as another *"burned out"* educator looking for another job and more money. You must overcome employers' negative expectations and objections toward educators by clearly communicating your transferable abilities and skills in the most positive terms possible. These assessment techniques are designed to do precisely that.

Chapter Eight

DEVELOP A
REALISTIC OBJECTIVE

Goals and objectives are statements of what you want to do in the future. When combined with an assessment of your interests, values, abilities and skills and related to specific jobs, they give your job search needed direction and meaning for the purpose of targeting specific employers. Without them, your job search may founder as you present an image of uncertainty and confusion to potential employers.

When you identify your strengths, you also create the necessary data base and vocabulary for developing your job objective. Using this vocabulary, you should be able to communicate to employers that you are a talented and purposeful individual who achieves *results*.

If you fail to do the preliminary self-assessment work necessary for developing a clear objective, you will probably wander aimlessly in the job market looking for interesting jobs you might fit into. Your goal, instead, should be to find a job or career that is compatible with your interests, motivations, skills, and talents as well as related to a vision of your future. In other words, try to find a job fit for you and your future rather than try to fit into a job that happens to be advertised and for which you think you can qualify.

EXAMINE YOUR PAST, PRESENT, AND FUTURE

Depending on how you approach your job search, your goals can be largely a restatement of your past MAS patterns or a vision of your future. If you base your job search on an analysis of your motivated abilities and skills, you may prefer restating your past patterns as your present and future goals. On the other hand, you may want to establish a vision of your future and set goals that motivate you to achieve that vision through a process of self-transformation.

The type of goals you choose to establish will involve different processes. However, the strongest goals will be those that combine your motivated abilities and skills with a realistic vision of your future.

> *The strongest goals will be those that combine your motivated abilities and skills with a realistic vision of your future.*

ORIENT YOURSELF TO EMPLOYERS' NEEDS

Your objective should be a concise statement of what you want to do and what you have to offer to an employer. The position you seek is *"what you want to do"*; your qualifications are *"what you have to offer"*. Your objective should state your strongest qualifications for meeting employer's needs. It should communicate what you have to offer an employer without emphasizing what you expect the employer to do for you. In other words, your objective should be *work-centered*, not self-centered; it should not contain trite terms which emphasize what you want, such as give me a(n) *"opportunity for advancement"*, *"position working with people"*, *"progressive company"*, or *"creative position"*. Such terms are viewed as *"canned"* job search language which say little of value about you. Above all, your objective should reflect your honesty and integrity; it should not be *"hyped"*.

Identifying what it is you want to do can be one of the most difficult job search tasks. Indeed, most job hunters lack clear objectives. Many engage in a random, and somewhat mindless, search for jobs by identifying available job opportunities and then adjusting their skills and objectives to fit specific job openings. While you will get a job using this approach, you may be misplaced and unhappy with what you find. You will fit into a job rather than find a job that is fit for you.

Knowing what you want to do can have numerous benefits. First, you define the job market rather than let it define you. The inherent fragmentation and chaos of the job market should be advantageous for you, because it enables you to systematically organize job opportunities around your specific objectives and skills. Second, you will communicate professionalism to prospective employers. They will receive a precise indication of your interests, qualifications, and purposes, which places you ahead of most other applicants. Third, being purposeful means being able to communicate to employers what you want to do. Employers are not interested in hiring indecisive and confused individuals. They want to know what it is you can do for them. With a clear objective, based upon a thorough understanding of your motivated skills and interests, you can take control of the situation as you demonstrate your value to employers.

Finally, few employers really know what they want in a candidate. Like most job seekers, employers lack clear employment objectives and knowledge about how the job market operates. If you know what you want and can help the employer define his or her *"needs"* as your objective, you will have achieved a tremendously advantageous position in the job market.

BE PURPOSEFUL AND REALISTIC

Your objective should communicate that you are a ***purposeful individual who achieves results***. It can be stated over different time periods as well as at various levels of abstraction and specificity. You can identify short, intermediate, and long-range objectives and very general to very specific objectives. Whatever the case, it is best to know your prospective audience before deciding on the type of objective. Your objective should reflect your career interests as well as employers' needs.

Objectives also should be ***realistic***. You may want to become President of the United States or solve all the world's problems. However, these objectives are probably unrealistic. While they may represent your ideals and fantasies, you need to be more realistic in terms of what you can personally accomplish in the immediate future. What, for example, are you prepared to deliver to prospective employers over the next few months? While it is good to set challenging objectives, you can overdo it. Refine your objective by thinking about the next major step or two you would like to make in your career advancement—not some grandiose leap outside reality!

Your objective should communicate that you are a purposeful individual who achieves results. It gives meaning and direction to all other activities.

PROJECT YOURSELF INTO THE FUTURE

Even after identifying your abilities and skills, specifying an objective can be the most difficult and tedious step in the job search process; it can stall the resume writing process indefinitely. This simple one-sentence, 25-word statement can take days or weeks to formulate and clearly define. Yet, it must be specified prior to writing the resume and engaging in other job search steps. An objective gives meaning and direction to all other activities.

Your objective should be viewed as a function of several influences. Since you want to build upon your strengths and you want to be realistic, your abilities and skills will play a central role in formulating your work objective. At the same time, you do not want your objective to become a function solely of your past accomplishments and skills. You may be very skilled in certain areas, but you may not want to use these skills in the future. As a result, your values and interests filter which skills you will or will not incorporate into your work objective.

Overcoming the problem of historical determinism—your future merely reflecting your past—requires incorporating additional components into defining your objective. One of the most important is your ideals, fantasies, or dreams. Everyone engages in these, and sometimes they come true. Your ideals, fantasies, or dreams may include making $1,000,000 by age 45; owning a Mercedes-Benz and a Porsche; taking trips to Rio, Hong Kong, and Rome; owning your own business; developing financial independence; writing a best-selling novel; solving major social problems; or winning the Nobel Peace Prize. If your fantasies require more money than you are now making, you will need to incorporate monetary considerations into your work objective. For example, if you have these fantasies, but your sense of realism tells you that your objective is to move from a $26,000 a year education position to a $28,000 a year position outside education you will be going nowhere, unless you can fast-track in your new position. Therefore, you will need to set a higher objective to satisfy your fantasies.

You can develop realistic objectives many different ways. We don't claim to have a new or magical formula, only one which has worked for many individuals. We assume you are capable of making intelligent career decisions if given sufficient data. Using redundancy once again, our approach is designed to provide you with sufficient corroborating data from several sources and perspectives so that you can make preliminary decisions. If you follow our steps in setting a realistic objective, you should be able to give your job search clear direction.

Four major steps are involved in developing a work objective. Each step can be implemented in a variety of ways:

STEP 1: Develop or obtain basic data on your functional/transferable skills, which we discussed in Chapter Five.

STEP 2: Acquire corroborating data about yourself from others, tests, and yourself. Several resources are available for this purpose:

A. **From others:** Ask three to five individuals whom you know well to evaluate you according to the questions in the *"Strength Evaluation"* form on page 128. Explain to these people that you believe their candid appraisal will help you gain a better understanding of your strengths and weaknesses from the perspectives of others. Make copies of this form and ask your evaluators to complete and return it to a designated third party who will share the information—but not the respondent's name—with you.

STRENGTH EVALUATION

TO: _____

FROM: _____

I am going through a career assessment process and thought you would be an appropriate person to ask for assistance. Would you please candidly respond to the questions below? Your comments will be given to me by the individual designed below; s/he will not reveal your name. Your comments will be used for advising purposes only. Thank you.

What are my strengths?

What weak areas might I need to improve?

In your opinion, what do I need in a job or career to make me satisfied?

Please return to: _____

B. **From vocational tests:** Although we prefer self-generated data, vocationally-oriented tests can help clarify, confirm, and translate your understanding of yourself into occupational directions. If you decide to use vocational tests, contact a professional career counselor who can administer and interpret the tests. We recommend several of the following tests:

- Strong-Campbell Interest Inventory
- Myers-Briggs Type Indicator
- Edwards Personal Preference Schedule
- Kuder Occupational Interest Survey
- APTICOM
- Jackson Vocational Interest Survey
- Ramak Inventory
- Vocational Interest Inventory
- Career Assessment Inventory
- Temperament and Values Inventory

C. **From yourself:** Numerous alternatives are available for you to practice redundancy. Refer to the exercises in Chapter Six that assist you in identifying your work values, job frustrations and dissatisfactions, things you love to do, things you enjoy most about work, and your preferred interpersonal environments.

STEP 3: Project your values and preferences into the future by completing simulation and creative thinking exercises:

A. **Ten Million Dollar Exercise:** First, assume that you are given a $10,000,000 gift; now you don't have to work. Since the gift is restricted to your use only, you cannot give any part of it away. What will you do with your time! At first? Later on? Second, assume that you are given another $10,000,000, but this time you are required to give it all away. What kinds of causes, organizations, charities, etc. would you support? Complete the following form in which you answer these questions:

WHAT WILL I DO WITH
TWO $10,000,000 GIFTS?

First gift is restricted to my use only:

_____

_____

_____

_____

_____

Second gift must be given away:

_____

_____

_____

_____

_____

_____

SOURCE: John C. Crystal, *"Life/Work Planning Workshop"*

B.   Obituary Exercise: Make a list of the most important things you would like to do or accomplish before you die. Two alternatives are available for doing this. First, make a list in response to this lead-in statement: *"Before I die, I want to..."*

BEFORE I DIE, I WANT TO . . .

1. _____
   _____

2. _____
   _____

3. _____
   _____

4. _____
   _____

5. _____
   _____

6. _____
   _____

7. _____
   _____

8. _____
   _____

9. _____
   _____

10. _____
    _____

Second, write a newspaper article which is actually your obituary for 10 years from now. Stress your accomplishments over the coming ten year period.

MY OBITUARY

Obituary for Mr./Ms. _____ to appear
in the _____ Newspaper in 2000.

_____

_____

_____

_____

_____

_____

_____

_____

_____

_____

_____

_____

_____

_____

_____

_____

_____

_____

_____

_____

C. **My Ideal Work Week:** Starting with Monday, place each day
of the week as the headings of seven sheets of paper. Develop
a daily calendar with 30-minute intervals, beginning at 7am and
ending at midnight. Your calendar should consist of a 118-hour
week. Next, beginning at 7am on Monday (sheet one), identify
the *ideal activities* you would enjoy doing, or need to do for
each 30-minute segment during the day. Assume you are
capable of doing anything; you have no constraints except

those you impose on yourself. Furthermore, assume that your work schedule consists of 40 hours per week. How will you fill your time? Be specific.

MY IDEAL WORK WEEK

Monday

am		pm	
7:00	_____	4:00	_____
7:30	_____	4:30	_____
8:00	_____	5:00	_____
8:30	_____	5:30	_____
9:00	_____	6:00	_____
9:30	_____	6:30	_____
10:00	_____	7:00	_____
10:30	_____	7:30	_____
11:00	_____	8:00	_____
11:30	_____	8:30	_____
12:00	_____	9:00	_____
p.m.	_____	9:30	_____
12:30	_____	10:00	_____
1:00	_____	10:30	_____
1:30	_____	11:00	_____
2:00	_____	11:30	_____
2:30	_____	12:00	_____
3:00	_____	Continue for Tuesday, Wednesday, Thursday, and Friday	
3:30	_____		

D. My Ideal Job Description: Develop your ideal future job. Be sure you include:

- Specific interests you want to build into your job.
- Work responsibilities.
- Working conditions.
- Earnings and benefits.
- Interpersonal environment.
- Working circumstances, opportunities, and goals.

Use *"My Ideal Job Specifications"* on page 135 to outline your ideal job. After completing this exercise, synthesize the job and write a detailed paragraph which describes the kind of job you would most enjoy:

DESCRIPTION OF MY IDEAL JOB

```
┌─────── DESCRIPTION OF MY IDEAL JOB ───────┐
│                                           │
│   ─────────────────────────────────────  │
│                                           │
│   ─────────────────────────────────────  │
│                                           │
│   ─────────────────────────────────────  │
│                                           │
│   ─────────────────────────────────────  │
│                                           │
│   ─────────────────────────────────────  │
│                                           │
│   ─────────────────────────────────────  │
│                                           │
│   ─────────────────────────────────────  │
│                                           │
└───────────────────────────────────────────┘
```

STEP 4: Test your objective against reality. Evaluate and refine it by conducting market research, a force field analysis, library research, and informational interviews.

A. **Market Research:** Four steps are involved in conducting this research:

    1. **Products or services:** Based upon all other assessment activities, make a list of what you *do* or *make*:

```
┌────────── PRODUCTS/SERVICES ──────────┐
│              I DO OR MAKE              │
│                                       │
│   1. _____   │
│                                       │
│   2. _____   │
│                                       │
│   3. _____   │
│                                       │
```

STEP 4: Test your objective against reality. Evaluate and refine it by conducting market research, a force field analysis, library research, and informational interviews.

A. Market Research: Four steps are involved in conducting this research:

1. Products or services: Based upon all other assessment activities, make a list of what you *do* or *make*:

PRODUCTS/SERVICES I DO OR MAKE

1. _____
2. _____
3. _____
4. _____
5. _____
6. _____
7. _____
8. _____
9. _____
10. _____

2. Market: Identify who needs, wants, or buys what you do or make. Be specific. Include individuals, groups, and organizations. Then, identify *what* specific *needs* your products or services fill. Next, assess the *results* you achieve with your products or services.

THE MARKET FOR MY PRODUCTS/SERVICES

Individuals, groups, organizations needing me:

1. _____
2. _____

3. _____

4. _____

5. _____

Needs I fulfill:

1. _____

2. _____

3. _____

4. _____

5. _____

Results/Outcomes/Impacts of my products/services:

1. _____

2. _____

3. _____

4. _____

5. _____

3. **New Markets:** Brainstorm a list of *who else* needs your products or services. Think about ways of expanding your market. Next, list any new needs your current or new market has which you might be able to fill:

DEVELOPING NEW NEEDS

Who else needs my products/services?

1. _____

2. _____

3. _____

4. _____

5. _____

New ways to expand my market:

1. _____

2. _____

3. _____

4. _____

5. _____

New needs I should fulfill:

1. _____

2. _____

3. _____

4. _____

5. _____

4. **New products and/or services:** List any new products or services you can offer and any new needs you can satisfy:

NEW PRODUCTS/
SERVICES I CAN OFFER

1. _____

2. _____

3. _____

4. _____

5. _____

NEW NEEDS I CAN MEET

1. _____

2. _____

3. _____

4. _____

5. _____

B. **Force Field Analysis:** Once you have developed a tentative or firm objective, force field analysis can help you understand the various internal and external forces affecting the achievement of your objective. Force field analysis follows a specific sequence of activities:

- Clearly state your objective or course of action.

- List the positive and negative forces affecting your objective. Specify the internal and external forces working *for* and *against* you in terms of who, what, where, when, and how much. Estimate the impact of each force upon your objective.

- Analyze the forces. Assess the importance of each force upon your objective and its probable affect upon you. Some forces may be irrelevant to your goal. You may need additional information to make a thorough analysis.

- Maximize positive forces and minimize negative ones. Identify actions you can take to strengthen positive forces and to neutralize, overcome, or reverse negative forces. Focus on the key forces which are real, important, and probable.

- Assess the feasibility of attaining your objective and, if necessary, modifying it in light of new information.

C. **Conduct Library Research:** This research should strengthen and clarify your objective. Consult various reference materials on alternative jobs and careers:

CAREER & JOB   • *Dictionary of Occupational Titles*
ALTERNATIVES: • *Encyclopedia of Careers and*

Vocational Guidance
- *Guide for Occupational Exploration*
- *Occupational Outlook Handbook*
- *Occupational Outlook Quarterly*

INDUSTRIAL
DIRECTORIES:
- *Bernard Klein's Guide to American Directories*
- *Dun and Bradstreet's Middle Market Directory*
- *Dun and Bradstreet's Million Dollar Directory*
- *Encyclopedia of Business Information Sources*
- *Geography Index*
- *Poor's Register of Corporations, Directors, and Executives*
- *Standard Directory of Advertisers*
- *The Standard Periodical Directory*
- *Standard and Poor's Industrial Index*
- *Standard Rate and Data Business Publications Directory*
- *Thomas' Register of American Manufacturers*

ASSOCIATIONS:
- *Directory of Professional and Trade Associations*
- *Encyclopedia of Associations*

GOVERNMENT
SOURCES:
- *The Book of the States*
- *Congressional Directory*
- *Congressional Staff Directory*
- *Congressional Yellow Book*
- *Federal Directory*
- *Federal Yellow Book*
- *Municipal Yearbook*
- *Taylor's Encyclopedia of Government Officials*
- *United National Yearbook*
- *United States Government Manual*

	• *Washington Information Directory*

NEWSPAPERS: • *The Wall Street Journal*
 • Major city newspapers
 • Trade newspapers
 • Any city newspaper—especially the Sunday edition.

BUSINESS PUBLICATIONS: • *Barron's, Business Week, Business World, Forbes, Fortune, Harvard Business Review, Money, Time, Newsweek, U.S. News and World Report*

OTHER LIBRARY RESOURCES: • Trade journals (refer to the *Directory of Special Libraries and Information Centers* and *Subject Collections: A Guide to Specialized Libraries of Businesses, Governments, and Associations*).
 • Publications of Chambers of of Commerce; State Manufacturing Associations; and federal, state, and local government agencies
 • Telephone books—The Yellow Pages
 • Trade books on *"How to get a job"*

4. **Conduct Informational Interviews:** This may be the most useful way to clarify and refine your objective. We'll discuss this procedure in subsequent chapters.

After completing these steps, you will have identified what it is you **can** do (abilities and skills), enlarged your thinking to include what it is you would **like** to do (aspirations), and probed the realities of implementing your objective. Thus, setting a realistic work objective is a function of the diverse considerations represented on page 143.

Your work objective is a function of both subjective and objective information as well as idealism and realism. We believe the strongest

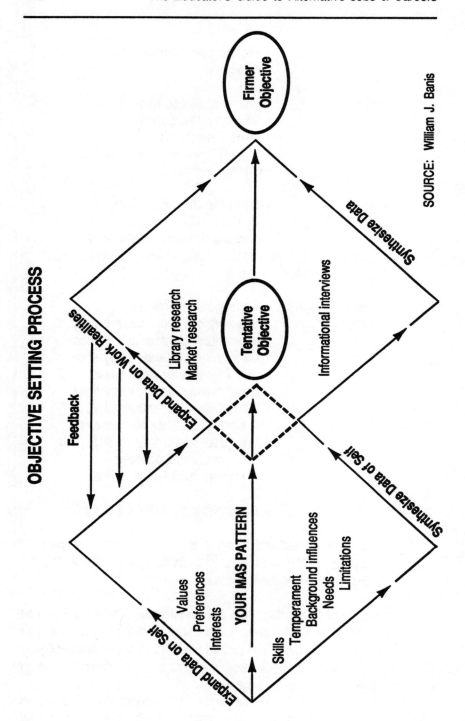

OBJECTIVE SETTING PROCESS

SOURCE: William J. Banis

emphasis should be placed on your competencies and should include a broad data-base. Your work objective is realistic in that it is tempered by your past experiences, accomplishments, skills, and current research. An objective formulated in this manner permits you to think beyond your past experiences.

> *Your work objective is realistic in that it is tempered by your past experiences, accomplishments, skills, and current research.*

STATE A FUNCTIONAL OBJECTIVE

Your job objective should be oriented toward skills and results or outcomes. You can begin by stating a functional job objective at two different levels: a general objective and a specific one for communicating your qualifications to employers both on resumes and in interviews. Thus, this objective setting process sets the stage for other key job search activities. For the general objective, begin with the statement:

STATING YOUR GENERAL OBJECTIVE

I would like a job where I can use my ability to _____ _____*which will result in* _____ _____ .

SOURCE: Richard Germann and Peter Arnold, *Bernard Haldane Associates Job & Career Building* (New York: Harper and Row, 1980), 54-55.

The objective in this statement is both a *skill* and an *outcome*. For example, you might state:

SKILLS-BASED AND
RESULTS-ORIENTED OBJECTIVE

I would like a job where my experience in program development, supported by innovative decision-making and systems engineering abilities, will result in an expanded clientele and a more profitable organization.

At a second level you may wish to re-write this objective in order to target it at various consulting firms. For example, on your resume it becomes:

JOB TARGETED OBJECTIVE

An increasingly responsible research position in consulting, where proven decision-making and system engineering abilities will be used for improving organizational productivity.

The following are examples of weak and strong objective statements. Various styles are also presented:

WEAK OBJECTIVES

Management position which will use business administration degree and will provide opportunities for rapid advancement.

A position in social services which will allow me to work with people in a helping capacity.

A position in Personnel Administration with a progressive firm.

Sales Representative with opportunity for advancement.

STRONGER OBJECTIVES

*To use computer science training in **software development** for designing and implementing operating systems.*

A public relations position which will maximize opportunities to develop and implement programs, to organize people and events, and to communicate positive ideas and images. Effective in public speaking and in managing a publicity/promotional campaign.

A position as a General Sales Representative with a pharmaceutical house which will use chemistry background and ability to work on a self-directed basis in managing a marketing territory.

A position in data analysis where skills in mathematics, computer programming, and deductive reasoning will contribute to new systems development.

Retail Management position which will use sales/customer service experience and creative abilities for product display and merchandising. Long term goal: Progression to merchandise manager with corporate-wide responsibilities for product line.

Responsible position in investment research and analysis. Interests and skills include securities analysis, financial planning, and portfolio management. Long range goal: to become a Chartered Financial Analyst.

It is important to relate your objective to your audience. While you definitely want a good job, your audience wants to know what you can do for them. Remember, your objective should be work-centered, not self-centered.

We will return to this discussion when we examine how to develop the objective section on your resume. Your objective will become the key element for organizing all other elements on your resume.

Chapter Nine

PRODUCE EFFECTIVE
RESUMES AND LETTERS

At every stage in the job search you must communicate a positive image to potential employers. The initial impression you make on an employer through applications, resumes, letters, telephone calls, or informational interviews will determine whether the employer is interested in interviewing you and offering you a position.

The fact that you are an educator is both a plus and minus for many employers. While you may think you are a good communicator, you may quickly discover your communication talent is most appropriate for the culture you normally operate within—fellow educators and students. Once you move outside education and begin communicating with other work cultures, your messages may be evaluated differently. Therefore, when looking for employment outside education, you need to communicate a positive image that will relieve any potential employer anxieties about hiring an ex-educator.

Developing and managing effective job search communication should play a central role in everything you do related to finding employment. While this communication will take several verbal and nonverbal forms, your first communication with employers will most likely be by letter, telephone, or in a face-to-face meeting. Job search letters often include your calling card—the resume. These documents are essentially nonverbal forms of communication that need to be both written and distributed with impact.

At every stage in the job search you must communicate a positive image to potential employers.

RESUMES FOR EDUCATORS

Writing resumes and letters for jobs outside education is a new and unfamiliar task for many educators. Elementary and secondary educators complete lengthy application forms for school boards in lieu of writing a resume. College and university educators write something approximating the normal resume. Known as vita, curriculum vita, or academic resumes, these documents tend to be lengthy, self-serving, and archaic obituaries which are incomprehensible to individuals outside education. Given the nature of these documents, it is surprising how colleges and universities can make informed staffing decisions!

The academic resume is unique and confined mainly to the halls of academia. Taken outside education, it is both pretentious and ineffective; it is one reason why non-educators have difficulty understanding what educators are capable of doing outside education. Academic resumes list teaching fields, publications, professional papers, positions, and a helter-skelter collection of other oddities which are supposed to *"impress"* as well as communicate something relevant to fellow educators. Indicative of the non-performance rank and status thinking of many educators, these resumes are bad habits that should be broken. As you look outside education for a job, hide your curriculum vita! Nobody wants it other than fellow educators. Instead, keep a clear and open mind, and begin by building upon your skills and job objective by writing an effective non-educational resume which will get you interviews. This chapter is designed to help you do precisely this.

WRITING RESUMES

Resumes are important tools for communicating your purpose and capabilities to employers. While many jobs only require a completed application form, you should always prepare a resume for influencing the hiring process. Application forms do not substitute for resumes.

Many myths surround resumes and letters. Some people still believe a resume should summarize one's history. Others believe it will get them a job. And still others believe they should be mailed in response to classified ads. The reality is this: A resume advertises your qualifications to prospective employers. It is your calling card for getting interviews.

A resume advertises your qualifications to prospective employers. It is your calling card for getting interviews.

Ineffective Resumes

Most people write ineffective resumes. Misunderstanding the purpose of resumes, they make numerous mistakes commonly associated with weak resumes and poor advertising copy. Their resumes often lack an objective, include unrelated categories of information, are too long, and appear unattractive. Other common pitfalls identified by employers include:

- Poor layout
- Misspellings and punctuation errors
- Poor grammar
- Unclear purpose
- Too much jargon
- Irrelevant data
- Too long or too short
- Poorly typed and reproduced
- Unexplained time gaps
- Too boastful

- Deceptive or dishonest
- Difficult to understand or interpret

Your resume, instead, should incorporate the characteristics of strong and effective resumes:

- Clearly communicate your purpose and competencies in relation to employers' needs.
- Be concise and easy to read.
- Motivate the reader to read it in-depth.
- Tell employers that you are a responsible and purposeful individual—a doer who can solve their problems.

Keep in mind that most employers are busy people who normally glance at a resume for only 20 to 30 seconds. Your resume, therefore, must sufficiently catch their attention to pass the 20 to 30 second evaluation test. When writing your resume, ask yourself the same question asked by employers: *"Why should I read this or contact this person for an interview?"* Your answer should result in an attractive, interesting, unique, and skills-based resume.

Employers are busy people who normally only glance at a resume for 20 or 30 seconds.

Types of Resumes

You have four types of resumes to choose from: chronological, functional, combination, or resume letter. Each format has various advantages and disadvantages, depending on your background and purpose. For example, someone first entering the job market or making a major career change should use a functional resume. On the other hand, a person who wants to target a particular job may choose to use a resume letter. Examples of these different types of resumes are included at the end of this chapter. Further assistance in developing each section of your resume is found in

Krannich's and Banis' comprehensive resume development book, *High Impact Resumes and Letters*. For numerous examples based upon these resume writing principles, examine the Krannichs' *Dynamite Resumes: 101 Great Examples!*

The *chronological resume* is the standard resume used by most applicants. It comes in two forms: traditional and improved. The *traditional chronological resume* is also known as the *"obituary resume"*, because it both *"kills"* your chances of getting a job and is a good source for writing your obituary. Summarizing your work history, this resume lists dates and names first and duties and responsibilities second; it includes extraneous information such as height, weight, age, marital status, sex, and hobbies. While relatively easy to write, this is the most ineffective resume you can produce. Its purpose at best is to inform people of what you have done in the past as well as where, when, and with whom. It tells employers little or nothing about what you want to do, can do, and will do for them. As an educator, this type of resume would tell employers that you are indeed an educator and that you probably want to remain so the rest of your life. This is the ultimate self-centered resume.

The *improved chronological resume* communicates directly to employers your purpose, past achievements, and probable future performance. You should use this type of resume when you have extensive experience directly related to a position you seek. This resume should include a work objective which reflects both your work experience and professional goals. The work experience section should include the names and addresses of former employers followed by a brief description of your accomplishments, skills, and responsibilities; inclusive employment dates should appear at the end. Do not begin with dates; they are the least significant element in the descriptions. Be sure to stress your *accomplishments* and *skills* rather than your formal duties and responsibilities. You want to inform your audience that you are a productive and responsible person who gets things done—a doer.

As an educator looking for employment outside education, you should avoid using a chronological resume. It is not appropriate for career changers. It communicates the wrong messages—you lack direct work experience or you have not advanced in your career. Instead, consider writing a functional or combination resume.

Functional resumes should be used by individuals making a significant career change, first entering the workforce, or re-entering the job market after a lengthy absence. This resume should stress your accomplishments and transferable skills regardless of previous work settings and job titles. This could include accomplishments as a teacher or volunteer worker.

Names of employers and dates of employment should not appear on this resume.

Functional resumes have certain weaknesses. While they are important bridges for the inexperienced and for those making a career change, some employers dislike these resumes. Since many employers still look for names, dates, and direct job experience, this resume does not meet their expectations. You should use a functional resume only if your past work experience does not strengthen your objective when making a major career change.

Functional resumes should be used by individuals making a significant career change.

Combination resumes are a compromise between chronological and functional resumes. Having more advantages than disadvantages, this resume may be exactly what you need as you attempt to relate your experience and skills as an educator to other worlds of work.

Combination resumes have the potential to both *meet* and *raise* the expectations of employers. You should stress your accomplishments and skills as well as include your work history. Your work history should appear as a separate section immediately following your presentation of accomplishments and skills in the *"Areas of Effectiveness"* or *"Experience"* section. It is not necessary to include dates unless they enhance your resume. This is the perfect resume for educators looking for jobs and careers outside education.

Resume letters are substitutes for resumes. Appearing as a job inquiry or application letter, resume letters highlight various sections of your resume, such as work history, experience, areas of effectiveness, objective, or education, in relation to employers' needs. These letters are used when you prefer not sending your more general resume. Resume letters have one major weakness: they give employers insufficient information and thus may prematurely eliminate you from consideration.

Structuring Resume Content

After choosing an appropriate resume format, you should generate the necessary information for structuring each category of your resume. You developed much of this information when you identified your motivated abilities and skills and specified your objective in Chapters Five through Eight. Include the following information on separate sheets of paper:

```
─────────── RESUME STRUCTURE ───────────
```

CONTACT INFORMATION:	name, address, and telephone number.
WORK OBJECTIVE:	refer to your data in Chapter Eight on writing an objective.
EDUCATION:	degrees, schools, dates, highlights, special training.
WORK EXPERIENCE:	paid, unpaid, civilian, military, and part-time employment. Include job titles, employers, locations, dates, skills, accomplishments, duties, and responsibilities. Use the functional language developed in Chapter Five.
OTHER EXPERIENCE:	volunteer, civic, and professional memberships. Include your contributions, demonstrated skills, offices held, names, and dates.
SPECIAL SKILLS OR LICENSES/ CERTIFICATES:	foreign languages, teaching, paramedical, etc. relevant to your objective.
MISCELLANEOUS INFORMATION:	references, expected salary, willingness to relocate and travel, availability dates, and other information supporting your objective.

Producing Drafts

Once you generate the basic data for constructing your resume, your next task is to reduce this data into draft resumes. If, for example, you write a combination resume, the internal organization of the resume should be as follows:

- Contact information
- Work objective
- Qualifications or functional experience
- Work history or employment
- Education

Be careful in including any other type of information on your resume. Other information most often is extraneous or negative information. You should only include information designed to strengthen your objective.

While your first draft may run more than two pages, try to get everything into one or two pages for the final draft. Most employers lose interest after reading the first page. If you produce a two-page resume, one of the best formats is to attach a single supplemental page to a self-contained one-page resume.

Your final draft should conform to the following rules for creating an excellent resume:

RULES FOR EFFECTIVE RESUMES

RESUME "DON'TS"

- ***Don't*** use abbreviations except for your middle name.
- ***Don't*** make the resume cramped and crowded; it should be pleasing to the eyes.
- ***Don't*** make statements you can't document.
- ***Don't*** use the passive voice.
- ***Don't*** change tense of verbs.
- ***Don't*** use lengthy sentences and descriptions.
- ***Don't*** refer to yourself as *"I"*.
- ***Don't*** include negative information.
- ***Don't*** include extraneous information.

RESUME "DOS"

- **Do** use action verbs and the active voice.
- **Do** be direct, succinct, and expressive with your language.
- **Do** appear neat, well organized, and professional.
- **Do** use ample spacing and highlights (all caps, underlining, bulleting) for different emphases.
- **Do** maintain an eye pleasing balance. Try centering your contact information at the top, keeping information categories on the left in all caps, and describing the categories in the center and on the right.
- **Do** check carefully your spelling, grammar, and punctuation.
- **Do** clearly communicate your purpose and value to employers.
- **Do** communicate your strongest points first.

Evaluating the Final Product

You should subject your resume drafts to two types of evaluations. An **Internal evaluation** consists of reviewing our lists of *"dos"* and *"don'ts"* to make sure your resume conforms to these rules. An **external evaluation** should be conducted by circulating your resume to three or more individuals whom you believe will give you frank, objective, and useful feedback. Avoid people who tend to flatter you. The best evaluator would be someone in a hiring position similar to one you will encounter in the actual interview. It's best to choose someone who is employed outside education. Ask these people to critique your draft resume and suggest improvements in both form and content. This will be your most important evaluation. After all, the only evaluation that counts is the one that helps get you an interview. Asking someone to critique your resume is one way to spread the word that you are job hunting. As we will see in Chapter Eleven, this is one method for getting invited to an interview!

Final Production

Your final resume can be typed, wordprocessed, or typeset. If you type it, be sure it looks professional. Use an electric typewriter with a carbon ribbon. Varying the typing elements and styles can produce an attractive copy. Do not use a portable typewriter with a nylon ribbon since it does not produce professional copy. Many typists will do your resume on the proper machine for $10 to $20.

If you have it wordprocessed, be sure the final copy is printed on a letter quality printer using a carbon ribbon or on a laser printer. Dot matrix and near letter quality printers make your resume look both unprofessional and mass produced.

Alternatively, you can have a printer typeset your resume. This may cost anywhere from $20 to $50. The final product should look first-class. However, it may look *too* professional or *too* slick; some employers may think you had someone else write the resume for you.

Whichever method you use, be sure to proofread the final copy. Many people spend good money on production only to later find typing errors.

When reproducing the resume, you must consider the quality and color of paper as well as the number of copies you need. By all means use good quality paper. You should use watermarked 20-pound or heavier bond paper. Costing 3¢ to 7¢ per sheet, this paper can be purchased through stationery stores and printers. It is important not to cut corners at this point by purchasing cheap paper or using copy machine paper. You may save $5 on 100 copies, but you also will communicate an unprofessional image to employers.

Use one of the following paper colors: white, off-white, light tan, light gray, or light blue. Avoid blue, yellow, green, pink, orange, red, or any other bright colors. Conservative, light-muted colors are the best. Any of these colors can be complemented with black ink. In the case of light gray—our first choice—a navy blue ink looks best. Dark brown ink is especially attractive on light tan paper.

Your choices of paper quality and color say something about your personality and professional style. They communicate nonverbally your potential strengths and weaknesses. Employers will use these as indicators for screening you in or out of an interview. At the same time, these choices may make your resume stand out from the crowd of standard black-on-white resumes.

You have two choices in reproducing your resume: a copy machine or an offset process. Many of the newer copy machines give good reproductions on the quality paper you need—nearly the same quality as the offset process. You should be able to make such copies for 10-20¢ per page. The offset process produces the best quality because it uses a printing plate. It also is relatively inexpensive—5 to 10¢ per copy with a minimum run of 100 copies. The cost per copy decreases with large runs of 300, 500, or 1000. In the end, you should be able to have your resume typed and 100 copies reproduced on high quality colored bond paper for less than $25. If you have it typeset, the same number of copies may cost you $50.

Whatever your choices, do not try to cut costs when it comes to producing your resume. It simply is not worth it. Remember, your resume is your calling card—it should represent your best professional image. Put your best foot forward at this stage. Go in style; spend a few dollars on producing a first-class resume.

Remember, your resume is your calling card—it should represent your best professional image.

JOB SEARCH LETTERS

Resumes sent through the mail are normally accompanied by a cover letter. After interviewing for information or a position, you should send a thank-you letter. Other occasions will arise when it is both proper and necessary for you to write different types of job search letters. Examples of these letters are presented *High Impact Resumes and Letters* and *Dynamite Cover Letters*.

Your letter writing should follow the principles of good resume and business writing. Job hunting letters are like resumes—they advertise you for interviews. Like good advertisements, these letters should follow four basic principles for effectiveness:

1. Catch the reader's attention.
2. Persuade the reader of your benefits or value.
3. Convince the reader with evidence.
4. Move the reader to acquire the product.

Basic Preparation Rules

Before you begin writing a job search letter, ask yourself several questions to clarify the content of your letter:

- *What is the **purpose** of the letter?*
- *What are the **needs** of my audience?*
- *What **benefits** will my audience gain from me?*
- *What is a good opening sentence or paragraph for grabbing the **attention** of my audience?*
- *How can I maintain the **interests** of my audience?*
- *How can I best end the letter so that the audience will be **persuaded** to contact me?*
- *If a resume is enclosed, how can my letter best **advertise the resume**?*
- *Have I spent enough **time** revising and proofreading the letter?*
- *Does the letter represent my **best professional effort**?*

Since your letters are a form of business communication, they should conform to the rules of good business correspondence:

PRINCIPLES OF GOOD BUSINESS COMMUNICATION

- Plan and organize what you will say by outlining the content of your letter.

- Know your purpose and structure your letter accordingly.

- Communicate your message in a logical and sequential manner.

- State your purpose immediately in the first sentence and paragraph; main ideas always go first.

- End your letter by stating what your reader can expect next from you.

- Use short paragraphs and sentences; avoid overly complex sentences.

- Punctuate properly and use correct grammar and spelling.

- Use simple and straight forward language; avoid jargon.

> • Communicate your message as directly and briefly as possible.

The rules stress how to both **organize and communicate** your message with impact. At the same time, you should always have a specific purpose in mind as well as know the needs of your audience.

Types of Letters

Cover letters provide cover for your resume. You should avoid overwhelming a one-page resume with a two-page letter or repeating the contents of the resume in the letter. A short and succinct one-page letter which highlights one or two points in your resume is sufficient. Three paragraphs will suffice. The first paragraph should state your interests and purposes for writing. The second paragraph should highlight your possible value to the employer. The third paragraph should state that you will call the individual at a particular time to schedule an interview.

However, do not expect great results from cover letters. Many professional job search firms use word processing equipment and mailing lists to flood the job market with resumes and cover letters. As a result, employers are increasingly suspicious of the authenticity of such letters.

Approach letters should get employers to engage in the 5R's of informational interviewing.

Approach letters are written for the purpose of developing job contacts, leads, or information as well as for organizing networks and getting interviews—the subjects of Chapter Eleven. Your primary purposes should be to get employers to engage in the 5R's of informational interviewing:

- **Reveal** useful information and advice.
- **Refer** you to others.
- **Read** and **revise** your resume.
- **Remember** you for future reference.

These letters help you gain access to the hidden job market.

Approach letters can be sent out *en masse* to uncover job leads, or they can target particular individuals or organizations. It is best to target these letters since they have maximum impact when personalized in reference to particular positions.

The structure of approach letters is similar to other letters. The first paragraph states your purpose. In so doing, you may want to use a personal statement for openers, such as *"Mary Tillis recommended that I write to you..."* or *"I am familiar with your..."* State your purpose, but do not suggest that you are asking for a job—only career advice or information. In your final paragraph, request a meeting and indicate you will call to schedule such a meeting at a mutually convenient time.

Thank-you letters may well become your most effective job search letters. They especially communicate your thoughtfulness. These letters come in different forms and are written for various occasions. The most common thank-you letter is written after receiving assistance, such as job search information or a critique of your resume. Other occasions include:

- **Immediately following an interview:** Thank the interviewer for the opportunity to interview for the position. Repeat your interest in the position.

- **Receive a job offer:** Thank the employer for his or her faith in you and express your appreciation.

- **Rejected for a job:** Thank the employer for giving you the *"opportunity"* to interview for the job. Ask to be remembered for future reference.

- **Terminate employment:** Thank the employer for the experience and ask to be remembered for future reference.

- **Begin a new job:** Thank the employer for giving you this new opportunity and express your confidence in producing the value he or she is expecting from you.

Several of these thank-you letters are unusual, but they all have the same goal in mind—to be remembered by potential employers in a positive light. In a job search, being remembered by employers is the closest thing to being invited to an interview and offered a job.

*Being remembered by employers is the
closest thing to being invited to
an interview and offered a job.*

DISTRIBUTION AND MANAGEMENT

The only good resumes are the ones that get read, remembered, referred, and result in a job interview. Therefore, after completing a first-rate resume and job search letters, you must decide what to do with them. Are you planning to only respond to classified ads? What other creative distribution methods might you use, such as sending it to friends, relatives, and former employers? What is the best way to proceed?

Responding to Classified Ads

Most of your writing activities should focus on the hidden job market. At the same time, you should respond to job listings in newspapers, magazines, and personnel offices. While this is largely a numbers game, you can increase your odds by the way you respond to the listings.

You should be selective in your responses. Since you know what you want to do, you will be looking for only certain types of positions. Once you identify them, your response entails little expenditure of time and effort—an envelope, letter, stamp, resume, and maybe 20 minutes of your time. You have little to lose. While you have the potential to gain by sending a letter and resume in response to an ad, remember the odds are usually against you.

It is difficult to interpret job listings. Some employers place blind ads with P.O. Box numbers in order to collect resumes for future reference. Others wish to avoid aggressive applicants who telephone or *"drop-in"* for interviews. Many employers work through professional recruiters who place these ads. While you may try to second guess the rationale behind such ads, respond to them as you would to ads with an employer's name, address, or telephone number. Assume there is a real job behind the ad.

Most ads request a copy of your resume. You should respond with a cover letter and resume as soon as you see the ad. Depending on how much information about the position is revealed in the ad, your letter should be tailored to emphasize your qualifications vis-a-vis the ad. Examine the ad carefully. Underline any words or phrases which relate to your qualifications. In your cover letter you should use similar terminology in emphasizing your qualifications. Keep the letter brief and to the point.

Keep your letter brief and concise
and highlight your qualifications
as stated in the employer's ad.

If the ad asks you to state your salary history or salary requirements, state *"negotiable"* or *"open"*. Alternatively, you can include a figure by stating a salary range 20 percent above your present salary base. For example, if you are making $30,000 a year, you can state this as *"in the $30,000 to $36,000 range"*. Use your own judgment in addressing the salary question. There is no hard and fast rule on stating a figure or range. A figure helps the employer screen-out individuals with too high a salary expectation. Keep salary considerations to the end of the interview—after you have demonstrated your value and have more information about the position.

You may be able to increase your odds by sending a second copy of your letter and resume two or three weeks after your initial response. Most applicants normally reply to an ad during the seven day period immediately after it appears in print. Since employers often are swamped with responses, your letter and resume may get lost in the crowd. If you send a second copy of your application two or three weeks later, the employer will have more time to give you special attention. By then, he or she also will have a better basis on which to compare you to the others.

Keep in mind that your cover letter and resume may be screened among 400 other resumes and letters. Thus, you want your cover letter to be eye catching and easy to read. Keep it brief and concise and highlight your qualifications as stated in the employer's ad. Don't spend a great deal of time responding to an ad or waiting anxiously at your mailbox or telephone for a reply. Keep moving on to other job search activities.

Self-Initiated Methods

Your letters and resumes can be distributed and managed in various ways. Many people shotgun hundreds of cover letters and resumes to prospective employers. This is a form of gambling where the odds are against you. For every 100 people you contact in this manner, expect one or two who might be interested in you. After all, successful direct-mail experts at best expect only a 2 percent return on their mass mailings!

If you choose to use the shotgun methods, you can increase your odds by using the *telephone*. Call the prospective employer within a week after he or she receives your letter. This technique will probably increase your effectiveness rate from 1 to 5 percent.

However, many people are shotgunning their resumes today. As more resumes and letters descend on employers with the increased use of word processing equipment, the effectiveness rates may be even lower. This also can be an expensive marketing method.

Your best distribution strategy will be your own modification of the following procedure:

1. Selectively identify whom you would be interested in working for.
2. Send an approach letter.
3. Follow up with a telephone call seeking an appointment for an interview.

In more than 50 percent of the cases, you will get an interview. It is best not to include a copy of your resume with the approach letter. Keep your resume for the end of the interview. Chapter Eleven outlines the procedures for conducting this informational interview.

Recordkeeping

Once you begin distributing letters and resumes, you also will need to keep good records for managing your job search writing campaign. Purchase file folders for your correspondence and notes. Be sure to make copies of all letters you write since you may need to refer to them over the telephone or before interviews. Record your activities with each employer—letters, resumes, telephone calls, interviews—on a 4 x 6 card and file it according to the name of the organization or individual. These files will help you quickly access information and enable you to evaluate your job search progress.

Always remember the purpose of resumes and letters—*advertise you for interviews*. They do not get jobs. Since most employers know nothing about you, *you must effectively communicate your value in writing prior to the critical interview*. While you should not overestimate the importance of this written communication, neither should you underestimate it.

TRADITIONAL CHRONOLOGICAL RESUME
(Obituary Type)

Karen Jones

Address: 1234 Main Street
Norfolk, VA 23508

Telephone: Area Code 804, Number 440-4321

Marital Status: Divorced; 2 children; ages 10 and 12
Date of Birth: April 1, 1952
Health: Excellent
Height: 5 feet, 4 inches
Weight: 125 lbs.

Educational Background:

University of Virginia, Charlottesville, Virginia. Bachelor of Arts Degree in English Literature with Certification in Secondary Education, June 1974.

Old Dominion University, Norfolk, Virginia. Master of Science Degree in Secondary Education, June 1979.

Work History:

1980 to Present—Norfolk Public Schools, Norfolk, VA.
English Teacher—I teach 11th and 12th grade English composition and creative writing classes. I have also served as co-director of the senior class play, coordinated student fund raising activities, and chaired the school committee which developed recruiting and public relations materials. I have given speeches at student events and helped write speeches for the school administration.

1975-1980—Full-time Homemaker.

1973-1975—Chesapeake Public Schools, Chesapeake, Virginia.
English Teacher—I taught 10th and 11th grade composition classes.

Community Involvements:

Toastmaster's International. Since 1979, I have been very active and have held a variety of chapter offices. During the past three years I have served as a district representative and officer.

Hobbies and Interests:

I enjoy physical exercise (running and racquetball), sailing, piano, theater, gardening, and gourmet cooking.

References:

Dr. James Smith, Superintendent of Norfolk Public Schools.
Mr. Robert Sinclair, Principal, Norfolk High School.
Mr. Paul Amos, Governor, Tidewater District, Toastmasters International.

IMPROVED CHRONOLOGICAL RESUME

KAREN JONES
1234 Main Street
Norfolk, Virginia 23508
Telephone 804-440-4321

OBJECTIVE: A public relations position involving program planning and coordination which requires an ability to work with diverse publics, develop publicity and promotional campaigns, market services and benefits, and meet deadlines.

WORK EXPERIENCE:

English Teacher: Norfolk Public Schools, Norfolk, Virginia.
Taught creative writing and composition. Organized and supervised numerous fund-raising projects which involved local businesses, media, parents, and students. Co-directed senior class pays. Wrote and gave several "keynote" speeches at special student programs. Served as school liaison to Parent-Teachers Association; designed a plan to increase membership and involve parents in school activities. Chaired city-wide public relations committee; coordinated development and production of promotional materials. Served as speech "ghost-writer" and editor for administrators. (1980 to present)

English Teacher: Chesapeake Public Schools, Chesapeake, Virginia.
Taught English composition. Write, designed, and developed multi-media instructional programs to interest students in writing. Served as advisor to student newspaper. (1974-1977)

ADDITIONAL EXPERIENCE:

Toastmasters International, Tidewater Chapter, Virginia.

District Representative: Elected to governing board of Southeast Virginia District. Served in liaison capacity between district officers and local chapter. Planned, organized, and publicized training workshops and regional competition. (1986 to present).

Chapter Officer (President, Treasurer, Sergeant-at-Arms):
Developed a publicity plan which increased membership by 20 percent. Kept financial records and prepared budget reports. Acquired extensive public speaking experience and training. (1982-1989)

EDUCATION:

M.S.Ed. in Secondary Education, 1979: Old Dominion University, Norfolk, Virginia.
B.A. in English Literature, 1974: University of Virginia, Charlottesville, Virginia.

FUNCTIONAL RESUME

KAREN JONES
1234 Main Street
Norfolk, Virginia 23508
Telephone 804-440-4321

OBJECTIVE: A public relations position involving program planning and coordination which requires an ability to work with diverse publics, develop publicity and promotional campaigns, market services and benefits, and meet deadlines.

AREAS OF EFFECTIVENESS

PLANNING AND COORDINATING
Organized and supervised several fund raising projects. Designed and implemented membership campaigns. Chaired public relations committee for school system; coordinated development and production of promotional materials. Publicized special events and programs to constituent groups. Developed multi-media instructional package to facilitate learning and involve students. Taught creative writing.

PROMOTING PUBLICIZING, MARKETING, AND WRITING
Developed promotional plan to attract new members to organizations. Coordinated publicity of special events and media. Wrote and edited speeches for self and school administrators. Helped design and produce promotional materials. Publicized special events and programs to constituent groups. Developed multi-media instructional package to facilitate learning and involve students. Taught creative writing.

COMMUNICATING AND INSTRUCTING
Gave numerous speeches over a seven year period to a variety of audiences. Conducted meetings and chaired committees. Coached administrators in writing and presenting speeches. Taught English for ten years in public schools.

EDUCATION: M.S.Ed., Old Dominion University, Norfolk, Virginia, 1979.
B.A., University of Virginia, Charlottesville, Virginia.

COMBINATION RESUME

KAREN JONES
1234 Main Street
Norfolk, Virginia 23508
Telephone 804-440-4321

OBJECTIVE: A public relations position involving program planning and coordination which requires an ability to work with diverse publics, develop publicity and promotional campaigns, market services and benefits, and meet deadlines.

AREAS OF EFFECTIVENESS

PLANNING AND COORDINATING   Organized and supervised several fund raising projects. Designed and implemented membership campaigns. Chaired public relations committee for school system; coordinated development and production of promotional materials. Publicized special events and programs to constituent groups. Developed multi-media instructional package to facilitate learning and involve students. Taught creative writing.

PROMOTING PUBLICIZING, MARKETING, AND WRITING   Developed promotional plan to attract new members to organizations. Coordinated publicity of special events and media. Wrote and edited speeches for self and school administrators. Helped design and produce promotional materials. Publicized special events and programs to constituent groups. Developed multi-media instructional package to facilitate learning and involve students. Taught creative writing.

COMMUNICATING AND INSTRUCTING   Gave numerous speeches over a seven year period to a variety of audiences. Conducted meetings and chaired committees. Coached administrators in writing and presenting speeches. Taught English for ten years in public schools.

WORK EXPERIENCE:

English Teacher: Norfolk Public Schools, Norfolk, Virginia.
Taught 11th and 12th grade creative writing and composition. (1980-present)

English Teacher: Chesapeake Public Schools, Chesapeake, Virginia.
Taught 10th and 11th grade composition. Advisor to student newspaper. (1974-1977).

EDUCATION:

M.S.Ed., Old Dominion University, Norfolk, Virginia, 1979.
B.A., University of Virginia, Charlottesville, Virginia.

RESUME LETTER

1234 Main Street
Norfolk, Virginia 23508
April 30, 199__

Mr. Dale Roberts, Business Manager
Virginia Beach Convention Center
Virginia Beach, Virginia 23519

Dear Mr. Roberts:

A mutual acquaintance of ours, Paul Amos, suggested that I contact you about the new Virginia Beach Convention Center. He remarked that you are developing a comprehensive public relations and marketing plan to attract convention business.

As an officer of my local chapter and regional division of Toastmasters International, I have acquired a substantial amount of public relations, special events planning, and program coordination experience. Along with my professional work, my background includes working with diverse audiences, developing publicity campaign and promotional materials, marketing services and benefits, recruiting new members, handling financial records, and meeting important deadlines. Furthermore, I have experience in writing and giving speeches, chairing work groups, representing organizations, creative writing, and teaching.

Since I have a strong interest in public relations-type activities and have a thorough knowledge of our region and its resources, I was quite interested to hear that your new marketing plan may use conference coordinators to work with your sales staff. I would be very interested in learning more about your plans and exploring future possibilities.

I plan to be near your office next week and wonder if we could have a brief meeting? I'll give your office a call in the next few days to see if a mutually convenient time could be arranged.

Sincerely,

Karen Jones

Chapter Ten

RESEARCH ALTERNATIVE
JOBS AND COMMUNITIES

The old adage that *"knowledge is power"* is especially true when conducting a job search. Your job search is only as good as the knowledge you acquire and use for finding the job you want.

Gathering, processing, and using information is the lifeblood of any job search. Research integrates the individual job search activities and provides feedback for adapting strategies to the realities of the job market. Given the numerous individuals and organizations involved in your job search, you must develop an information gathering strategy that will help you gain knowledge about, as well as access to, those individuals and organizations that will play the most important role in your job search.

RESEARCH PURPOSES

Research is the key to gathering, processing, and using information in your job search. It is a skill that will point you in fruitful directions for minimizing job search frustrations and maximizing successes. Be sure to make research one of your top priorities.

However, most people are reluctant to initiate a research campaign which involves using libraries and telephoning and meeting new people.

Such reluctance is due in part to the lack of knowledge on how to conduct research and where to find resources, and in part to a certain cultural shyness which inhibits individuals from initiating contacts with strangers. However, research is not a difficult process. After all, most people conduct research daily as they read and converse with others about problems. This daily research process needs to be specified and focused on your job search campaign. As an educator, you should be particularly adept at conducting the research necessary for an effective job search campaign.

Research serves several purposes when adapted to your job search. First, knowing the who, what, when, and where of organizations and individuals is essential for targeting your resume and conducting information-al and job interviews. Second, the research component should broaden your perspective on the job market in relationship to your motivated abilities and skills and job objective. Since there are over 20,000 different job titles as well as several million job markets, even a full-time research campaign will uncover only a small segment of the job market relevant to your interests and skills.

A third purpose of research is to better understand how to relate your motivated abilities and skills to specific jobs and work environment. Once you research and understand the critical requirements of a given job in a specific work environment, you can assess the appropriateness of that job for you vis-a-vis your pattern of motivated abilities and skills (MAS).

Fourth, researching organizations and individuals should result in systematically uncovering a set of contacts for developing your jobs search network. One of your major research goals should be to compile names, addresses, and telephone numbers of individuals who may become important resources in your new network of job contacts.

A fifth purpose of research is to learn the *languages* of alternative jobs and careers. While educators' disciplines have specialized languages, jargon, and vocabularies, so do disciplines, jobs, and careers outside education. You can learn to better converse in these languages by reading trade journals, annual reports, pamphlets, and other organizational literature as well as talking with people in various occupational fields. Knowing these languages—especially asking and answering intelligent questions in the language of the employer—is important for conducting successful referral and job interviews.

Finally, research should result in bringing some degree of structure, coherence, and understanding to the inherently decentralized, fragmented, and chaotic job market. Without research, you place yourself at the mercy of chance and luck; thus, you become a subject of your environment. Research best enables you to take control of your situation. It is power.

Your research activities should focus on four major targets: occupational alternatives, organizations, individuals, and communities. If you give equal time to all four, you will be well on your way to getting job interviews and offers.

INVESTIGATE ALTERNATIVE JOBS AND CAREERS

Your initial research should help familiarize you with *job and career alternatives* to education, the subject of Chapter Three. For example, the U.S. Department of Labor identifies approximately 20,000 job titles. Most individuals are occupationally illiterate and unaware of the vast array of available jobs and careers. Therefore, it is essential to investigate occupational alternatives in order to broaden your perspective on the job market.

As reviewed in Chapter Three, you should start your research by examining several key directories that provide information on alternative jobs and careers:

- *The Occupational Outlook Handbook*
- *Occupational Outlook Handbook*
- *Encyclopedia of Careers and Vocational Guidance*
- *Guide to Occupational Exploration*

You will also find several books that focus on alternative jobs and careers. National Textbook Company, for example, publishes one of the most comprehensive series of books on alternative jobs and careers. Their books now address 138 different job and career fields. Representative titles in their *"Opportunities in..."* series include:

- *Opportunities in Advertising*
- *Opportunities in Airline Careers*
- *Opportunities in Banking*
- *Opportunities in Business Management*
- *Opportunities in Child Care*
- *Opportunities in Craft Careers*
- *Opportunities in Electrical Trades*
- *Opportunities in Eye Care*
- *Opportunities in Gerontology*

- *Opportunities in Interior Design*
- *Opportunities in Laser Technology*
- *Opportunities in Microelectronics*
- *Opportunities in Optometry*
- *Opportunities in Pharmacy*
- *Opportunities in Public Relations*
- *Opportunities in Robotics*
- *Opportunities in Sports and Athletics*
- *Opportunities in Telecommunications*

National Textbook also publishes another useful set of books in a *"Careers in..."* series:

- *Careers in Accounting*
- *Careers in Business*
- *Careers in Communications*
- *Careers in Computers*
- *Careers in Education*
- *Careers in Engineering*
- *Careers in Health Care*
- *Careers in Science*

Also look for eight volumes in the *"Career Directory"* series published by Career Press:

- *Advertising Career Directory*
- *Book Publishing Career Directory*
- *Business and Finance Career Directory*
- *Magazine Publishing Career Directory*
- *Marketing Career Directory*
- *Newspaper Publishing Career Directory*
- *Public Relations Career Directory*
- *Travel and Hospitality Career Directory*

Walker and Company publishes a *"Career Choices"* series of books closely linked to disciplines and majors in higher education:

- *Career Choices: Art*
- *Career Choices: Business*
- *Career Choices: Communications and Journalism*

- *Career Choices: Computer Science*
- *Career Choices: Economics*
- *Career Choices: English*
- *Career Choices: History*
- *Career Choices: Law*
- *Career Choices: Mathematics*
- *Career Choices: MBA*
- *Career Choices: Political Science and Government*
- *Career Choices: Psychology*

Facts on File publishes a few books on alternative jobs and careers in the communication and entertainment industries:

- *Career Opportunities in Art*
- *Career Opportunities in the Music Industry*
- *Career Opportunities in Television, Cable, and Video*
- *Career Opportunities in Writing*

Impact Publications publishes five volumes on international and public service careers:

- *The Almanac of International Jobs and Careers*
- *The Complete Guide to International Jobs and Careers*
- *The Almanac of American Government Jobs and Careers*
- *The Complete Guide to Public Employment*
- *Find a Federal Job Fast!*

Many other books examine a wide range of jobs and careers. Some are annual or biannual reviews of today's most popular jobs. You should find several of these books particularly helpful:

- *American Almanac of Jobs and Salaries*, John W. Wright (Avon).
- *Jobs 1991*, Ross and Kathryne Petras (Simon and Schuster).
- *101 Careers*, Michael Harkavy (Wiley).
- *Careers Encyclopedia*, Craig T. Norback ed. (National Textbook)
- *Top Professions*, Nicholas Basta (Petersons)
- *Great Careers*, Devon Cottrell Smith, ed. (Garrett Park Press).
- *The Jobs Rated Almanac*, Les Krantz (St. Martins Press).

If you are unable to find these books in your local library or bookstore, they can be ordered directly from Impact Publications. Order information is found at the end of this book. You may also want to request a copy of their free catalog of over 1,000 annotated job and career resources which includes these titles.

TARGET ORGANIZATIONS

After completing research on occupational alternatives, you should identify specific organizations which you are interested in learning more about. Next compile lists of names, addresses, and telephone numbers of important individuals in each organization. Also, write and telephone the organizations for information, such as an annual report and recruiting literature. The most important information you should be gathering concerns the organizations' goals, structures, functions, problems, and projected future opportunities and development. Since you invest part of your life in such organizations, treat them as you would a stock market investment. Compare and evaluate different organizations.

Several directories will assist you in researching organizations. Most are available in the reference sections of libraries:

- *Directory of American Firms Operating in Foreign Countries*
- *The Directory of Corporate Affiliations: Who Owns Whom*
- *Dun & Bradstreet's Middle Market Directory*
- *Dun & Bradstreet's Million Dollar Directory*
- *Dun & Bradstreet's Reference Book of Corporate Managements*
- *Encyclopedia of Business Information Sources*
- *Fitch's Corporation Reports*
- *MacRae's Blue Book*
- *Moody's Manuals*
- *The Multinational Marketing and Employment Directory*
- *Standard & Poor's Industrial Index*
- *Standard Rate and Data Business Publications Directory*
- *Thomas' Register of American Manufacturers*

Peterson's Guides publishes two annual directories that are the definitive guides to organizations that hire business, liberal arts, engineering, science, and computer graduates:

- *Job Opportunities for Business and Liberal Arts Graduates*
- *Job Opportunities for Engineering, Science, and Computer Graduates*

The following trade books identify organizations that are considered to be some of the best to work for today:

- *The 100 Best Companies to Work For in America*
- *The Almanac of American Employers*
- *The Best Companies for Women*

If you are interested in jobs with a particular organization, you should contact the personnel office for information on the types of jobs offered within the organization. You may be able to examine vacancy announcements which describe the duties and responsibilities of specific jobs. If you are interested in working for federal, state, or local governments, each agency will have a personnel office which can supply you with descriptions of their jobs. While gathering such information, be sure to ask people about their jobs.

CONTACT INDIVIDUALS

While examining directories and reading books on alternative jobs and careers will provide you with useful job search information, much of this material may be too general for specifying the right job for you. In the end, the best information will come directly from people in specific jobs in specific organizations. To get this information you must interview people. You especially want to learn more about the people who make the hiring decisions.

You might begin your investigations by contacting various professional and trade associations for detailed information on jobs and careers relevant to their members. For names, addresses, and telephone numbers of such associations, consult the following key directories which are available in most libraries:

- *The Encyclopedia of Associations* (Gale Research)
- *National Trade and Professional Associations* (Columbia Books)

Your most productive research activity will be talking to people. Informal, word-of-mouth communication is still the most effective channel of job search information. In contrast to reading books, people have more current, detailed, and accurate information. Ask them about:

- Occupational fields
- Job requirements and training
- Interpersonal environments
- Performance expectations
- Their problems
- Salaries
- Advancement opportunities
- Future growth potential of the organization
- How best to acquire more information and contacts
  in a particular field

You may be surprised how willingly friends, acquaintances, and strangers will give you useful information. But before you talk to people, do your library research so that you are better able to ask thoughtful questions.

ASK THE RIGHT QUESTIONS

The quality of your research will only be as good as the questions you ask. Therefore, you should focus on a few key questions that will yield useful information for guiding your job search. Answers to these questions will help make important job search decisions relevant to informational and job interviews.

Who Has the Power to Hire?

Finding out who has the power to hire may take some research effort on your part. Keep in mind that personnel offices normally do not have the power to hire. They handle much of the paper work involved in announcing vacancies, taking applications, testing candidates, screening credentials, and placing new employees on the payroll. In other words, personnel offices tend to perform auxiliary support functions for those who do the actual hiring—usually individuals in operating units.

If you want to learn who really has the power to hire, you need to conduct research on the particular organization that interests you. You should ask specific questions concerning who normally is responsible for various parts of the hiring process:

- Who describes the positions?
- Who announces vacancies?
- Who receives applications?
- Who administers tests?
- Who selects eligible candidates?
- Who chooses whom to interview?
- Who offers the jobs?

If you ask these questions about a specific position you will quickly identify who has what powers to hire. Chances are the power to hire is **shared** between the personnel office and the operating unit. You should not neglect the personnel office, and in some cases it will play a powerful role in all aspects of the hiring. Your research will reveal to what degree the hiring function has been centralized, decentralized, or fragmented within a particular organization.

How Does Organization X Operate?

It's best to know something about the internal operation of an organization before joining it. You research may uncover information that would convince you that a particular organization is not one in which you wish to invest your time and effort. You may learn, for example, that Company X has a history of terminating employees before they become vested in the company retirement system. Or Company X may be experiencing serious financial problems. Or advancement within Company X may be very political and company politics is vicious and debilitating.

You can get financial information about most companies by examining their annual reports as well as by talking to individuals who know the organization well. Information on the internal operations, especially company politics and power, must come from individuals who work within the organization. Ask them: *"Is this a good organization to work for?"* and let them expand on specific areas you wish to probe—advancement opportunities, working conditions, relationships among co-workers and supervisors, growth patterns, internal politics, management style, work values, opportunities for taking initiative.

What Do I Need to Do To
Get A Job With Organization X?

The best way to find how to get a job in a particular organization is to follow the advice in the next chapter on prospecting, networking, and informational interviewing. This question can only be answered by talking to people who know both the formal and informal hiring practices.

You can get information on the formal hiring system by contacting the personnel office. A telephone call should be sufficient to get this information.

But you must go beyond the formal system and personnel office in order to learn how best to conduct your job search. This means contacting people who know how one really gets hired in the organization, which may or may not follow the formal procedures. The best sources of information will be individuals who play a major role in the hiring process.

IDENTIFY THE RIGHT COMMUNITY

Your final research target is central to all other research targets and it may occur at any stage in your research. Identifying the geographical area where you would like to work will be one of your most important decisions. Once you make this decision, other job search decisions and activities become easier. For example, if you live in a small college town, you will probably need to move in order to change careers. If you are a member of a two-career family, opportunities for both you and your spouse will be greater in a growing metropolitan area. If you decide to move to another community, you will need to develop a long-distance job search campaign which has different characteristics from a local campaign. It involves writing letters, making long-distance phone calls, and visiting a community for strategic one to two-week periods during your vacations.

Deciding where you want to live involves researching various communities and comparing advantages and disadvantages of each. In addition to identifying specific job alternatives, organizations, and individuals in the community, you need to do research on other aspects of the community. After all, you will live in the community, buy or rent a residence, perhaps send children to school, and participate in community organizations and events. Often these environmental factors are just as important to your happiness and well-being as the particular job you accept. For example, you may be leaving a $30,000 a year academic job for a position in your favorite community—San Francisco. But you may quickly find you are worse off with your new $42,000 a year job, because you must pay $325,000 for a home in San Francisco that is nearly identical to the $120,000 home in your college-town community. Consequently, it would be foolish for you to take a new job without first researching several facets of the community in addition to job opportunities.

Research on different communities can be initiated form your local library. While most of this research will be historical in nature, several resources will provide you with a current profile of various communities. Statistical overviews and comparisons of states and cities are found in the *U.S. Census Data, The Book for the States,* and the *Municipal Yearbook.* Many libraries have a reference section of telephone books on various cities. If this section is weak or absent in your local library, contact your local telephone company.They have a relatively comprehensive library of telephone books. In addition to giving you names, addresses, and telephone numbers, the Yellow Pages are invaluable sources of information on the specialized structures of the public and private sectors of individual communities. The library may also have state and community directories as well as subscriptions to some state and community magazines and city newspapers. Research magazine, journal, and newspaper articles on different communities by consulting references in the *Reader's Guide to Periodical Literature,* the *Social Science and Humanities Index,* the *York Times Index,* and the *Wall Street Journal Index.*

For recent rankings of cities for identifying the best places to live, be sure to consult the latest edition of Richard Boyer and David Savageau's *Places Rated Almanac.* Joseph and Amy Lombardo's *The Job Belt* identifies the 50 best places in American for finding high-quality employment. Jill Andresky Fraser's *The Best U.S. Cities for Working Women* identifies the top 70 U.S. cities for women.

You should also consult several city job banks that will give you contact information on specific employers in major metropolitan communities. Bob Adams, Inc. publishes *The National Job Bank* as well as 17 job bank guides:

- *The Atlanta Job Bank*
- *The Boston Job Bank*
- *The Chicago Job Bank*
- *The Dallas/Fort Worth Job Bank*
- *The Denver Job Bank*
- *The Detroit Job Bank*
- *The Florida Job Bank*

- *The Houston Job Bank*
- *The Los Angeles Job Bank*
- *The Minneapolis Job Bank*
- *The New York Job Bank*
- *The Ohio Job Bank*
- *The Philadelphia Job Bank*
- *The San Francisco Job Bank*
- *The Seattle Job Bank*
- *The St. Louis Job Bank*
- *The Metropolitan Washington, DC Job Bank*

Surrey Books also publishes a similar job bank series for nine major metropolitan areas:

- *How to Get a Job in Atlanta*
- *How to Get a Job in Chicago*
- *How to Get a Job in Dallas/Ft. Worth*
- *How to Get a Job in Houston*
- *How to Get a Job in Los Angeles/San Diego*
- *How to Get a Job in New York*
- *How to Get a Job in San Francisco*
- *How to Get a Job in Seattle/Portland*
- *How to Get a Job in Washington, DC*

After narrowing down the number of communities that interest you, further research them in depth. Ask your relatives, friends, and acquaintances for contacts in the particular community; they may know people whom you can write or telephone for information and referrals. Once you have decided to focus on one community, visit it in order to establish personal contacts with key reference points, such as the local Chamber of Commerce, real estate firms, schools, libraries, churches, Forty-Plus Club (if appropriate), government agencies, and business firms and associations. Begin developing personal networks based upon the research and referral strategies in the next chapter. Subscribe to the local newspaper and to any community magazines which help profile the community. Follow the help-wanted, society, financial, and real estate sections of the newspaper—especially the Sunday edition. Keep a list of names of individuals who appear to hold influential community positions; you may want to contact these people for referrals. Write letters to set up informational interviews with key people; give yourself two months of lead time to complete your letter writing campaign. Your overall community research should focus on developing personal contacts which may assist you in both your job search and your personal move to the community.

KNOW WHAT'S IMPORTANT

Reviewing published resources can be extremely time consuming if taken to the extreme. While you should examine several of them, do not spend an inordinate amount of time reading and taking notes. Your time will be best spent in gathering information through meetings and conversations with key people. Your primary goals in conducting research should be identifying people to contact, setting appointments, and asking the right questions which lead to more information and contacts. If you engage in these activities you will know what is important when conducting research.

As you get further into your job search, networking for information, advice, and referrals will become an important element in your overall job search strategy. At that time you will come into closer contact with potential employers who can provide you with detailed information on their organizations and specific jobs. If you have a well defined MAS, specific job objectives, and a well focused resume, you should be in a good position to make networking pay off with useful information, advice, and referrals. You will quickly discover that the process of linking your MAS and objectives to specific jobs is an ongoing one involving several steps in your job search.

Chapter Eleven

NETWORK FOR INFORMATIONAL INTERVIEWS

Now that you have identified your skills, specified your objective, written your resume, and conducted research, what should you do next? At this point let's examine where you are going so you don't get preoccupied with the trees and thus lose sight of the larger forest. Let's identify the most effective methods for linking your previous job search activities to job interviews and offers.

FOCUS ON GETTING INTERVIEWS

Everything you do up to this point in your job search should be aimed at *getting a job interview.* The skills you identified, the goals you set, the resume you wrote, and the information you gathered are carefully related to one another so you will have maximum impact for communicating your qualifications to employers who, in turn, will decide to invite you to a job interview.

But there are secrets to getting a job interview you should know before continuing further with your job search. The most important secret is the informational interview—a type of interview which yields useful job search information and may lead to job interviews and offers. Based on prospecting and networking techniques, these interviews minimize rejections and competition as well as quickly open the doors to organizations and employers. If you want a job interview, you first need to understand the informational interview and how to initiate and use it for maximum impact.

PROSPECTING AND NETWORKING

What do you do after you complete your resume? Most people send cover letters and resumes in response to job listings; they then wait to be called for a job interview. Viewing the job search as basically a direct-mail operation, many are disappointed in discovering the realities of direct-mail— a 5 percent response rate is considered outstanding!

Successful job seekers break out of this relatively passive job search role by orienting themselves toward face-to-face action. Being proactive, they develop interpersonal strategies in which the resume plays a supportive rather than a central role in the job search. They first present themselves to employers; the resume appears only at the end of a face-to-face conversation.

Throughout the job search you will acquire useful names and addresses as well as meet people who will assist you in contacting potential employers. Such information and contacts become key building blocks for generating job interviews and offers.

The most effective means of communication
are face-to-face and word-of-mouth.

Since the best and most numerous jobs are found on the hidden job market, you must use methods appropriate for this job market. Indeed, research and experience clearly show the most effective means of communication are face-to-face and word-of-mouth. The informal, interpersonal system of communication is the central nervous system of the hidden job market. Your goal should be to penetrate this job market with proven methods for success. Appropriate methods for making important job contacts are *prospecting and networking*. Appropriate methods for getting these contacts to provide you with useful job information are *informational and referral interviews*.

COMMUNICATE YOUR QUALIFICATIONS

Taken together, these interpersonal methods help you *communicate your qualifications to employers*. Although many job seekers—and especially educators who believe people get jobs and advance their careers on the basis of merit and qualifications rather than whom you know—may be reluctant to use this informal communication system, they greatly limit their potential for success if they do not.

Put yourself in the position of the employer for a moment. You have a job vacancy to fill. If you advertise the position, you may be bombarded with hundreds of resumes, applications, phone calls, faxes, and walk-ins. While you do want to hire the best qualified individual for the job, you simply don't have time nor patience to review scores of applications. Even if you use a P.O. Box number, the paperwork may quickly overwhelm you. Furthermore, with limited information from application forms, cover letters, and resumes, you find it hard to identify the best qualified individuals to invite for an interview; many look the same on paper. And people changing careers, such as educators, may not really *"fit"* properly into your expectations of someone with direct work experience relevant to a job you are trying to fill.

So what do you do? You might hire a professional job search firm to take on all of this additional work. On the other hand, you may want to better control the hiring process, especially since it appears to be filled with uncertainty and headaches. You want to minimize your risks and time so you can get back to what you do best—accomplishing the external goals of the organization. Like many other employers, you begin by calling your friends, acquaintances, and other business associates and ask if they or someone else might know of any good candidates for the position. If they can't help, you ask them to give you a call should they learn of anyone qualified for your vacancy. You, in effect, create your own hidden job market—an informal information network for locating desirable candidates. Your trusted contacts initially screen the candidates in the process of referring them to you. This both saves you time and minimizes your risks in hiring a stranger.

Based on this understanding of the employer's perspective, what should you do to best improve your chances of getting an interview and job offer?

Networking for information, advice, and referrals should play a central role in your overall job search. Remember, employers need to solve personnel problems. By conducting *informational interviews and networking* you help employers identify their needs, limit their alternatives, and thus make decisions and save money. Most important, such interviews and networking activities help relieve their anxiety of hiring an ex-educator.

At the same time, you gain several advantages by conducting these interviews:

1. You are less likely to encounter rejections since you are not asking for a job—only information, advice, referrals, and to be remembered.

2. You go after high level positions.

3. You encounter little competition.

4. You go directly to the people who have the power to hire.

5. You are likely to be invited to job interviews based upon the referrals you receive.

Most employers want more information on candidates to supplement the *"paper qualifications"* represented in application forms, resumes, and letters. Studies show that employers in general seek candidates who have these skills: communication, problem solving, analytical, assessment, and planning—key skills of educators. Surprising to many job seekers, technical expertise ranks third or fourth in employers' lists of most desired skills. These findings support a frequent observation made by employers: the major problems with employees relate to communication, problem solving, and analysis; individuals get fired because of political and interpersonal conflicts rather than technical incompetence.

Employers seek individuals they *like* both personally and professionally. Therefore, communicating your qualifications to employers entails more than just informing them of your technical competence. You must communicate that you have the requisite personal *and* professional skills for performing the job. Informal prospecting, networking, and informational interviewing activities are the best methods for communicating your *"qualifications"* to employers.

Employers seek individuals they like both personally and professionally.

DEVELOP NETWORKS

Networking is the process of purposefully developing relations with others. Networking in the job search involves connecting and interacting with other individuals who can be helpful to you. Your network consists of you interacting with these other individuals. The more you develop, maintain, and expand your networks, the more successful should be your job search.

Your network is your interpersonal environment. While you know and interact with hundreds of people, on a day-to-day basis you may encounter no more than 20 people. You frequently contact these people in face-to-face situations. Some people are more **important** to you than others. You **like** some more than others. And some will be more **helpful** to you in your job search than others. Your basic network may encompass the following individuals and groups: friends, acquaintances, immediate family, distant relatives, professional colleagues, spouse, supervisor, fellow workers, close friends and colleagues, and local businessmen and professionals, such as your banker, lawyer, doctor, minister, and insurance agent. You should contact many of these individuals for advice relating to your job search.

You need to **identify everyone in your network** who might help you with your job search. You first need to expand your basic network to include individuals you know and have interacted with over the past 10 or more years. Make a list of at least 200 people you know. Include friends and relatives from your Christmas card list, past and present neighbors, former classmates, politicians, business persons, previous employers, professional associates, ministers, insurance agents, lawyers, bankers, doctors, dentists, accountants, and social acquaintances.

After identifying your extended network, you should try to **link your network to others' networks**. The figure on page 188 illustrates this linage principle. Individuals in these other networks also have job information and contacts. Ask people in your basic network for referrals to individuals in their networks. This approach should greatly enlarge your basic job search network.

LINKING YOUR NETWORKS TO OTHERS

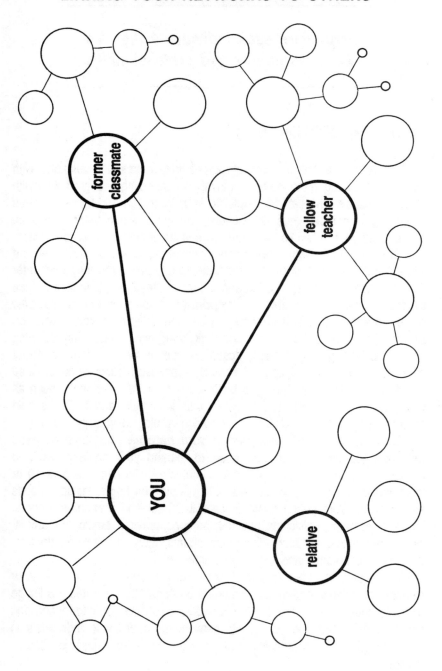

What do you do if individuals in your immediate and extended network cannot provide you with certain job information and contacts? While it is much easier and more effective to meet new people through personal contacts, on occasion you may need to **approach strangers without prior contacts**. In this situation, try the *"cold turkey"* approach. Write a letter to someone you feel may be useful to your job search. Research this individual so you are acquainted with their background and accomplishments. In the letter, refer to their accomplishments, mention your need for job information, and specify a date and time you will call to schedule a meeting. Another approach is to introduce yourself to someone by telephone and request a meeting and/or job information. While you may experience rejections in using these approaches, you also will experience successes. And those successes should lead to further expansion of your job search network.

PROSPECT FOR LEADS

The key to successful networking is an active and routine **prospecting campaign**. Salespersons in insurance, real estate, Amway, Shaklee, and other direct-sales businesses understand the importance and principles of prospecting; indeed, many have turned the art of prospecting into a science! The basic operating principle is **probability**: the number of sales you make science. The basic operating principle is **probability**: the number of sales you make is a direct function of the amount of effort you put into developing new contacts and following-through. Expect no more than a 10 percent acceptance rate: for every 10 people you meet, 9 will reject you and 1 will accept you. Therefore, the more people you contact, the more acceptances you will receive. If you want to be successful, you must collect many more *"nos"* than *"yeses"*. In a 10 percent probability situation, you need to contact 100 people for 10 successes.

These prospecting principles are extremely useful for making a career change. Like sales situations, the job search is a highly ego-involved activity often characterized by numerous rejections accompanied by a few acceptances. While no one wants to be rejected, few people are willing and able to handle more than a few rejections. They take a *"no"* as a sign of personal failure—and quit prematurely. If they persisted longer, they would achieve success after a few more *"nos"*. Furthermore, if their prospecting activities were focused on gathering information rather than making sales, they would considerably minimize the number of rejections. Therefore, this is what you should do:

- Prospect for job leads.
- Accept rejections as part of the game.
- Link prospecting to informational interviewing.
- Keep prospecting for more information and *"yeses"* which will eventually translate into job interviews and offers.

The job search is a highly ego-involved activity often characterized by numerous rejections accompanied by a few acceptances.

A good prospecting pace as you start your search is to make two new contacts each day. Start by contacting people in your immediate network. Let them know you are conducting a job search, but emphasize that you are only doing research. Ask for a few moments of their time to discuss your information needs. You are only seeking *information and advice* at this time—not a job.

It should take you about 20 minutes to make a contact by letter or telephone. If you make two contacts each day, by the end of the first week you will have 10 new contacts for a total investment of less than seven hours. By the second week you may want to increase your prospecting pace to four new contacts each day or 20 each week. The more contacts you make, the more useful information, advice, and job leads you will receive. If your job search bogs down, you probably need to increase your prospecting activities.

Expect each contact to refer you to two or three others who will also refer you to others. Consequently, your contacts should multiply considerably within only a few weeks.

HANDLE AND MINIMIZE REJECTIONS

These prospecting and networking methods are effective. While they are responsible for building, maintaining, and expanding multi-million dollar businesses, they work extremely well for job hunters. But they only work if you are patient and persist. *The key to networking success is to focus on gathering information while also learning to handle rejections.* Learn from rejections, forget them, and go on to more productive networking activities. The major reason direct-sales people fail is because they don't persist. The reason they don't persist is because they either can't take, or get tired of taking, rejections.

Rejections are no fun, especially in such an ego-involved activity as a job search. But you will encounter rejections as you travel on the road toward job search success. This road is strewn with individuals who quit prematurely because they were rejected four or five times. Don't be one of them!

Our prospecting and networking techniques differ from sales approaches in one major respect: we have special techniques for minimizing the number of rejections. If handled properly, at least 50 percent—maybe as many as 90 percent—of your prospects will turn into *"yeses"* rather than *"nos"*. The reason for this unusually high acceptance rate is how you introduce and handle yourself before your prospects. Many insurance agents and direct distributors expect a 90 percent rejection rate, because they are trying to sell specific products potential clients may or may not need. Most people don't like to be put on the spot—especially when it is in their own home or office—to make a decision to buy a product.

PRACTICE THE 5-R's

The principles of selling yourself in the job market are similar. People don't want to be put on the spot. They feel uncomfortable if they think you expect them to give you a job. Thus, you should never introduce yourself to a prospect by asking them for a job or a job lead. You should do just the opposite: relieve their anxiety by mentioning that you are not looking for a job from them—only job information and advice. You must be honest and sincere in communicating these intentions to your contact. The biggest turn-off for individuals targeted for informational interviews is insincere job seekers who try to use this as a mechanism to get a job.

Your approach to prospects must be subtle, honest, and professional. You are seeking *information, advice, and referrals* relating to several subjects: job opportunities, your job search approach, your resume, and others who may have similar information, advice, and referrals. Most people gladly volunteer such information. They generally like to talk about themselves, their careers, and others. They like to give advice. This approach flatters individuals by placing them in the role of the expert-advisor. Who doesn't want to be recognized as an expert-advisor, especially on such a critical topic as one's employment?

This approach should yield a great deal of information, advice, and referrals from your prospects. One other important outcome should result from using this approach: people will *remember* you as the person who made them feel at ease and who received their valuable advice. If they hear of job opportunities for someone with your qualifications, chances are they will contact you with the information. After contacting 100 prospects, you will have created 100 sets of eyes and ears to help you in your job search!

The best way to get a job is to ask for job information, advice, and referrals; never ask for a job.

The guiding principle behind prospecting, networking, and informational interviews is this: the best way to get a job is to ask for job information, advice, and referrals; never ask for a job. Remember, you want your prospects to engage in the 5-R's of informational interviewing:

- *Reveal* useful information and advice.
- *Refer* you to others.
- *Read* and *revise* your resume.
- *Remember* you for future reference.

If you follow this principle, you should join the ranks of thousands of successful job seekers who paid a great deal of money learning it from highly-paid professionals.

APPROACH KEY PEOPLE

Whom should you contact within an organization for an informational interview? Contact people who are busy, who have the power to hire, and who are knowledgeable about the organization. The least likely candidate will be someone in the personnel department. Most often the heads of operating units are the most busy, powerful, and knowledgeable individuals in the organization. However, getting access to such individuals may be difficult. Some people at the top may appear to be informed and powerful, but they may lack information on the day-to-day personnel changes or their influence is limited in the hiring process. It is difficult to give one best answer to this question.

Therefore, we recommend contacting a variety of people. Aim for the busy, powerful, and informed, but be prepared to settle for less. Secretaries, receptionists, and the person you want to meet may refer you to others. From a practical standpoint, you may have to take whomever you can schedule an appointment with. Sometimes people who are not busy can be helpful. Talk to a secretary or receptionist sometime about their boss or working in the organization. You may be surprised with what you learn!

Nonetheless, you will conduct informational interviews with different types of people. Some will be friends, relatives, or acquaintances. Others will be referrals or new contacts. You will gain the easiest access to people you already know. This can usually be done informally by telephone. You might meet at their home or office or at a restaurant.

You should use a more formal approach to gain access to referrals and new contacts. The best way to initiate a contact with a prospective employer is to *send an approach letter*. This letter should include the following elements:

OPENERS: If you have a referral, tell the individual you are considering a career in _____. His or her name was given to you by _____ who suggested he or she might be a good person to give you useful information about careers in _____. Should you lack a referral to the individual and thus must use a *"cold turkey"* approach to making this contact, you might begin your letter by stating that you are aware he or she has been at the forefront of _____ business—or whatever is both truthful and appropriate for the situation. A subtle form of flattery will be helpful at this stage.

REQUEST: Demonstrate your thoughtfulness and courtesy rather than aggressiveness by mentioning that you know he or she is busy. You hope to schedule a mutually convenient time for a brief meeting to discuss your questions and career plans. Most people will be flattered by such a request and happy to talk with you about their work—if they have time and are interested in you.

CLOSINGS: In closing the letter, mention that you will call the person to see if an appointment can be arranged. Be specific by stating the time and day you will call—for example, Thursday at 2pm. You must take the initiative in this manner to follow-up the letter with a definite contact time. If you don't, you cannot expect to hear from the person. It is *your* responsibility to make the telephone call to schedule a meeting.

ENCLOSURE: Do *not* enclose your resume with this approach letter. You should take your resume to the interview and present it as a topic of discussion near the end of your meeting. If you send it with the approach letter, you communicate a mixed and contradictory message. Remember your purpose for this interview: to gather information and advice. You are not—and never should be—asking for a job. A resume in a letter appears to be an application or a request for a job.

Many people will meet with you, assuming you are sincere in your approach. On the other hand, many people also are very busy and simply don't have the time to meet with you. If the person puts you off when you telephone for an appointment, clearly state your purpose and emphasize that you are not looking for a job with this person—only information and advice. If the person insists on putting you off, make the best of the situation: try to conduct the informational interview over the telephone.

Alternatively, write a nice thank-you letter in which you again state your intended purpose; mention your disappointment in not being able to learn from the person's experience; and ask to be remembered for future reference. Enclose your resume with this letter.

While you are ostensibly seeking information and advice, treat this meeting as an important preliminary interview. You need to communicate your qualifications—that you are competent, intelligent, honest, and likeable. These are the same qualities you should communicate in a formal job interview. Hence, follow the same advice given for conducting a formal interview and dressing appropriately for face-to-face meeting (Chapter Twelve).

CONDUCT THE INTERVIEW WELL

An informational interview will be relatively unstructured compared to a formal job interview. Since you want the interviewer to advise you, you reverse roles by asking questions which should give you useful information. You, in effect, become the interviewer. You should structure this interview with a particular sequence of questions. Most questions should be open-ended, requiring the individual to give specific answers based upon his or her experience.

The structure and dialogue for the informational interview might go something like this. You plan to take no more than 45 minutes for this interview. The first three to five minutes will be devoted to small talk—the weather, traffic, the office, mutual acquaintances, or an interesting or humorous observation. Since these are the most critical moments in the interview, be especially careful how you communicate nonverbally. Begin your interview by stating your appreciation for the individual's time:

"I want to thank you again for scheduling this meeting with me. I know you're busy. I appreciate the special arrangements you made to see me on a subject which is very important to my future."

Your next comment should be a statement reiterating your purpose as stated in your letter:

"As you know, I am exploring job and career alternatives. I know what I do well and what I want to do. But before I commit myself to a new job, I need to know more about various career options. I

thought you would be able to provide me with some insights into career opportunities, job requirements, and possible problems or promising directions in the field of _____."

This statement normally will get a positive reaction from the individual who may want to know more about what it is you want to do. Be sure to clearly communicate your job objective. If you can't, you may communicate that you are lost, indecisive, or uncertain about yourself. The person may feel you are wasting his or her time.

Your next line of questioning should focus on *"how"* and *"what"* questions centering on (1) specific jobs and (2) the job search process. Begin by asking about various aspects of specific jobs:

- Duties and responsibilities.
- Knowledge, skills, and abilities required.
- Work environment relating to fellow employees, work flows, deadlines, stress, initiative.
- Advantages and disadvantages.
- Advancement opportunities and outlook.
- Salary ranges.

Be a good listener, but make sure you move along with the questions.

Your informer will probably take a great deal of time talking about his or her experience in each area. Be a good listener, but make sure you move along with the questions.

Your next line of questioning should focus on your job search activities. You need as much information as possible on how to:

- Acquire the necessary skills.
- Best find a job in this field.
- Overcome any objections employers may have to your background.
- Uncover job vacancies which may be advertised.

- Develop job leads.
- Approach prospective employers.

Your final line of questioning should focus on your resume. Do not show your resume until you focus on this last set of questions. The purpose of these questions is to: (1) get the individual to read your resume in-depth, (2) acquire useful advice on how to strengthen it, (3) refer you to prospective employers, and (4) be remembered. With the resume in front of you and your interviewee, ask the following questions:

- *Is this an appropriate type of resume for the jobs I have outlined?*
- *If an employer received this resume in the mail, how do you think he or she would react to it?*
- *What do you see as possible weaknesses or areas that need to be improved?*
- *What should I do with this resume? Shotgun it to hundreds of employers with a cover letter? Use resume letters instead?*
- *What about the length, paper quality and color, layout, and typing? Are they appropriate?*
- *How might I best improve the form and content of the resume?*

You should receive useful advice on how to strengthen both the content and use of your resume. Most important, these questions force the individual to **read** your resume which, in turn, may be **remembered** for future reference.

Your last question is especially important in this interview. You want to be both **remembered** and **referred**. Some variation of the following question should help:

"I really appreciate all this advice. It is very helpful and it should improve my job search considerably. Could I ask you one more favor? Do you know two or three other people who could help me with my job search? I want to conduct as much research as possible, and their advice might be helpful also."

Before you leave, mention one more important item:

"During the next few months, should you hear of any job opportunities for someone with my interests and qualifications, I would

*appreciate being kept in mind. And please feel free to pass my name
on to others."*

Send a nice thank-you letter within 48 hours of completing this
informational interview. Express your genuine gratitude for the individual's
time and advice. Reiterate your interests, and ask to be remembered and
referred to others.

Follow-up on any useful advice you receive, particularly referrals. Approach referrals in the same manner you approached the person who gave
you the referral. Write a letter requesting a meeting. Begin the letter by
mentioning:

*"Mr./Ms. _____ suggested that I contact you concerning my
research on careers in _____."*

If you continue prospecting, networking, and conducting informational
interviews, soon you will be busy conducting interviews and receiving job
offers. While 100 informational interviews over a two-month period should
lead to several formal job interviews and offers, the pay-offs are uncertain
because job vacancies are unpredictable. We know cases where the first
referral turned into a formal interview and job offer. More typical cases
require constant prospecting, networking, and informational interviewing
activities. The telephone call or letter inviting you to a job interview can
come at any time. While the timing may be unpredictable, your persistent
job search activities will be largely responsible for the final outcome.

TELEPHONE FOR JOB LEADS

Telephone communication should play an important role in prospecting,
networking, and informational interviews. However, controversy centers
around how and when to use the telephone for generating job leads and
scheduling interviews. Some people recommend writing a letter and waiting
for a written or telephone reply. Others suggest writing a letter and following
it with a telephone call. Still others argue you should use the telephone
exclusively rather than write letters.

How you use the telephone will indicate what type of job search you are
conducting. Exclusive reliance on the telephone is a technique used by
highly formalized job clubs which operate phone banks for generating job
leads. Using the Yellow Pages as the guide to employers, a job club

member may call as many as 50 employers a day to schedule job interviews. A rather aggressive yet typical telephone dialogue goes something like this:

"Hello, my name is Jim Morgan. I would like to speak to the head of the training department. By the way, what is the name of the training director?"

"You want to talk to Ms. Stevens. Her number is 723-8191 or I can connect you directly."

"Hello, Ms. Stevens. My name is Jim Morgan. I have several years of training experience as both a trainer and developer of training materials. I'd like to meet with you to discuss possible openings in your department for someone with my qualifications. Would it be possible to see you on Friday at 2pm?"

Not surprising, this telephone approach generates many *"nos"*. If you have a hard time handling rejections, this telephone approach will help you confront your anxieties. The principle behind this approach is *probability*: for every 25 telephone *"nos"* you receive, you will probably get one or two *"yeses"*. Success is just 25 telephone calls away! If you start calling prospective employers at 9am and finish your 25 calls by 12 noon, you should generate at least one or two interviews. That's not bad for three hours of job search work. It beats a direct-mail approach.

While the telephone is more efficient than writing letters, its effectiveness is questionable. When you use the telephone in this manner, you are basically asking for a job. You are asking the employer: *"Do you have a job for me?"* There is nothing subtle or particularly professional about this approach. It is effective in uncovering particular types of job leads for particular types of individuals. If you need a job—any job—in a hurry, this is one of the most efficient ways of finding employment. It sure beats standing in line at the state employment office! However, if you are more concerned with finding a job that is right for you—a job you do well and enjoy doing, one that is fit for you—this telephone approach is inappropriate.

You must use your own judgment in determining when and how to use the telephone in your job search. There are appropriate times and methods for using the telephone, and these should relate to your job search goals and needs. We prefer the more conventional approach of writing a letter requesting an informational interview and following it up with a telephone call. While you take the initiative in scheduling an appointment, you do not put the individual on the spot by asking for a job. You are only seeking information and advice. This low-keyed approach results in numerous acceptances and has a higher probability of paying off with interviews than the aggressive telephone request. You should be trying to uncover jobs that are right for you rather than any job that happens to pop up from a telephoning blitz.

USE JOB CLUBS AND SUPPORT GROUPS

The techniques outlined thus far are designed for individuals conducting a self-directed job search. Job clubs and support groups are two important alternatives to these techniques.

Job clubs are designed to provide a group structure and support system to individuals seeking employment. These groups consist of about 12 individuals who are led by a trained counselor and supported with telephones, copying machines, and a resource center.

Highly formalized job clubs, such as the 40-Plus Club, organize job search activities for both the advertised and hidden job markets. As outlined by Azrin and Besalel in their book *Job Club Counselor's Manual*, job club activities include:

- Signing commitment agreements to achieve specific job search goals and targets.
- Contacting friends, relatives, and acquaintances for job leads.
- Completing activity forms.
- Using telephones, typewriters, photocopy machines, postage, and other equipment and supplies.
- Meeting with fellow participants to discuss job search progress.
- Telephoning to uncover job leads.
- Researching newspapers, telephone books, and directories.
- Developing research, telephone, interview, and social skills.
- Writing letters and resumes.
- Responding to want ads.
- Completing employment applications.

In other words, the job club formalizes many of the prospecting, networking, and informational interviewing activities within a group context and interjects the role of the telephone as the key communication device for developing and expanding networks.

Job clubs place excessive reliance on using the telephone for uncovering job leads. Members call prospective employers and ask about job openings. The Yellow Pages become the job hunting bible. During a two-week period, a job club member might spend most of his or her mornings telephoning for job leads and scheduling interviews. Afternoons are normally devoted to job interviewing.

We do not recommend joining such job clubs for obvious reasons. Most job club methods are designed for the hardcore unemployed or for individuals who need a job—any job—quickly. Individuals try to fit into available vacancies; their objectives and skills are of secondary concern. We recommend conducting your own job search or forming a support group which adapts some job club methods to our central concept of finding a job fit for you—one appropriate to your objective and in line with your particular mix of skills, abilities, and interests.

Support groups are a useful alternative to job clubs. They have one major advantage: they may cut your job search time in half. Forming or joining one of these groups can help direct as well as enhance your individual job search activities.

Your support group should consist of three or more individuals who are job hunting. Try to schedule regular meetings with specific purposes in mind. While the group may be highly social, especially if it involves close friends, it also should be *task-oriented*. Meet at least once a week and include your spouse. At each meeting set *performance goals* for the week. For example, your goal can be to make 20 new contacts and conduct five informational interviews. The contacts can be made by telephone, letter, or in person. Share your experiences and job information with each other. *Critique* each other's progress, make suggestions for improving the job search, and develop new strategies together. By doing this, you will be gaining valuable information and feedback which is normally difficult to gain on one's own. This group should provide important psychological supports to help you through your job search. After all, job hunting can be a lonely, frustrating, and exasperating experience. By sharing your experiences with others, you will find you are not alone. You will quickly learn that rejections are part of the game. The group will encourage you, and you will feel good about helping others achieve their goals. Try building small incentives into the group, such as the individual who receives the most job interviews for the month will be treated to dinner by other members of the group.

Chapter Twelve

INTERVIEWS, JOB OFFERS, AND SALARY NEGOTIATIONS

Make no mistake—the job interview is *the* most important step in the job search process. All previous job search activities lead to this one. Put simply, no interview, no job offer; no job offer, no negotiations, no salary, and no job.

Your previous job search activities have assisted you in getting this far, but the interview itself will determine whether you will be invited to a second interview and offered a position. How you approach the interview will make a difference in the outcome of the interview. Therefore, you need to know what best to do and not to do in order to make a good impression on your prospective employer.

INTERVIEWING FOR THE JOB

Nearly 95 percent of all organizations require job interviews prior to hiring employees. In fact, employers consider an effective interview to be the most important hiring criteria—outranking grade point average, related work experience, and recommendations.

While the job interview is the most important job search activity, it also is the most stressful job search experience. Your application, resume, and letters may get you to the interview, but you must perform well in person in order to get a job offer. Knowing the stakes are high, most people face interviews with dry throats and sweaty palms; it is a time of great stress. You will be on stage, and you are expected to put on a good performance.

How do you prepare for the interview? First, you need to understand the nature and purpose of the interview. Second, you must prepare to respond to the interview situation and the interviewer. Make sure whoever assists you in preparing for the interview evaluates your performance. Practice the whole interviewing scenario, from the time you enter the door until you leave. You should sharpen your nonverbal communication skills and be prepared to give positive answers to questions as well as ask intelligent questions. The more you practice, the better prepared you will be for the real job interview.

COMMUNICATION

An interview is a two-way communication exchange between an interviewer and interviewee. It involves both verbal and nonverbal communication. While we tend to concentrate on the content of what we say, research shows that approximately 65 percent of all communication is nonverbal. Furthermore, we tend to give more credibility to nonverbal than to verbal messages. Regardless of what you say, how you dress, sit, stand, use your hands, move your head and eyes, and listen communicate both positive and negative messages.

Job interviews can occur in many different settings and under various circumstances. You will write job interview letters, schedule interviews by telephone, be interviewed over the phone, and encounter one-on-one as well as panel, group, and series interviews. Each situation requires a different set of communication behaviors. For example, while telephone communication is efficient, it may be ineffective for interview purposes. Only certain types of information can be effectively communicated over the telephone because this medium limits nonverbal behavior. Honesty, intelligence, and likability—three of the most important values you want to communicate to employers—are primarily communicated nonverbally. Therefore, you should be very careful of telephone interviews—whether giving or receiving them.

Job interviews have different purposes and can be negative in many ways. From your perspective, the purpose of an initial job interview is to get a second interview, and the purpose of the second interview is to get a job offer. However, for many employers, the purpose of the interview is to eliminate you from a second interview or job offer. The interviewer wants to know why he or she should *not* hire you. The interviewer tries to do this by identifying your weaknesses. These differing purposes can create an adversarial relationship and contribute to the overall interviewing stress experienced by both the applicant and the interviewer.

Since the interviewer wants to identify your weaknesses, you must counter by *communicating your strengths* to lessen the interviewer's fears of hiring you. Recognizing that you are an unknown quantity to the employer, you must raise the interviewer's expectations of you.

You should prepare for the interview as if it were a $1,000,000 prize.

ANSWERING QUESTIONS

Hopefully your prospecting, networking, informational interviewing, and resume and letter writing activities result in several invitations to interview for jobs appropriate to your objective. Once you receive an invitation to interview, you should do a great deal of work in preparation for your meeting. You should prepare for the interview as if it were a $1,000,000 prize. After all, that may be what you earn with the employer over the next 20 years.

The invitation to interview will most likely come by telephone. In some cases, a preliminary interview will be conducted by telephone. The employer may want to shorten the list of eligible candidates from 10 to 3. By calling each individual, the employer can quickly eliminate marginal candidates as well as up-date the job status of each individual. When you get such a telephone call, you have no time to prepare. You may be dripping wet as you step from the shower or you may have a splitting headache as you pick up the phone. Telephone interviews always seem to occur at bad times. Whatever your situation, put your best foot forward based upon your thorough preparation for an interview. You may want to keep a list of questions near the telephone just in case you receive such a telephone call.

Telephone interviews often result in a face-to-face interview at the employer's office. Once you confirm an interview time and place, you should do as much research on the organization and employer as possible as well as learn to lessen your anxiety and stress levels by practicing the interview situation. **Preparation and practice** are the keys to doing your best.

During the interview, you want to impress upon the interviewer your knowledge of the organization by asking intelligent questions and giving intelligent answers. Your library and networking research should yield useful information on the organization and employer. Be sure you know something about the organization. Interviewers are normally impressed by interviewees who demonstrate knowledge and interest in their organization.

You should practice the actual interview by mentally addressing several questions most interviewers ask. Most of these questions will relate to your educational background, work experience, career goals, personality, and related concerns. The most frequently asked questions include:

Education

- Describe your educational background.
- Why did you attend _____ University (College or School)?
- Why did you major in _____?
- What was your grade point average?
- What subjects did you enjoy the most? The least? Why?
- What leadership positions did you hold?
- How did you finance your education?
- If you started all over, what would you change about your education?
- Why were your grades so low? So high?
- Did you do the best you could in school? If not, why not?

Work Experience

- What were your major achievements in each of your past jobs?
- Why did you change jobs before?
- What is your typical workday like?
- What functions do you enjoy doing the most?
- What did you like about your boss? Dislike?
- Which job did you enjoy the most? Why? Which job did you enjoy the least? Why?
- Have you ever been fired? Why?

Career Goals

- Why do you want to join our organization?
- Why do you think you are qualified for this position?
- Why are you looking for another job?
- Why do you want to make a career change?
- What ideally would you like to do?
- Why should we hire you?
- How would you improve our operations?
- What do you want to be doing five years from now?
- How much do you want to be making five years from now?
- What are your short-range and long-range career goals?
- If you could choose your job and organization, where would you go?
- What other types of jobs are you considering? Other companies?
- When will you be ready to begin work?
- How do you feel about relocating, traveling, working over-time, and spending weekends in the office?
- What attracted you to our organization?

Personality and Other Concerns

- Tell me about yourself.
- What are your major weaknesses? Your major strengths?
- What causes you to lose your temper?
- What do you do in your spare time? Any hobbies?
- What types of books do you read?
- What role does your family play in your career?
- How well do you work under pressure? In meeting deadlines?
- Tell me about your management philosophy.
- How much initiative do you take?
- What types of people do you prefer working with?
- How _____(creative, analytical, tactful, etc.) are you?
- If you could change your life, what would you do differently?

Your answers to each question should be positive and emphasize your **strengths**. Remember, the interviewer wants to know about your **weaknesses**. For example, if you are asked *"What are your weaknesses?"*, you can turn this potential negative question into a positive by answering something like this:

> *"I sometimes get so involved with my work that I neglect my family as well as forget to complete work around the house. My problem is that I'm somewhat of a workaholic."*

What employer could hold this negative against you? You have taken a negative and raised the expectations of the employer by basically saying you are a hard and persistent worker; the organization will get more for its money than expected.

When answering these and other questions, both the **substance** and **form** of your answers should be positive. For example, such words as *"couldn't"*, *"can't"*, *"won't"*, and *"don't"* may create a negative tone and distract rom the positive and enthusiastic image you are trying to create. While you cannot eliminate all negative words, at least recognize that the type of words you use makes a difference and therefore word choice should be better managed. Compare your reactions to the following interview answers:

QUESTION: "Why are you leaving education?"

ANSWER 1: *"I can't make ends meet any longer on an educator's salary and I don't see my circumstances getting any better."*

ANSWER 2: *"Although I have enjoyed my work in education, I am ambitious and feel that opportunities for growth and advancement would be greater elsewhere."*

Which one has the greatest impact in terms of projecting positives and strengths?

In addition to choosing positive words, selection **content information** which is positive and **adds** to the interviewer's knowledge about you. Avoid simplistic *"yes/no"* answers; they say nothing about you. Instead, provide information which explains your reasons and motivations behind specific events or activities. For example, how do you react to these two factual answers?

QUESTION: **"I see from your resume that you taught at Smith High School. Are you one of the faculty being affected by the recent budget cuts?"**

ANSWER 1: *"Yes, that's correct."*

ANSWER 2: *"Yes. Like many others, I've been affected by the recent budget cuts. However, instead of looking at my situation as a crisis, I'm approaching it as an opportunity to explore several other strong interests of mine. I know my talents can be useful in any number of settings, and I'm particularly interested in the work your department does."*

The significance of managing these and other interview questions with positive information can be illustrated with some examples. Let's assume that you are a secondary English teacher with 10 years of public school experience. You now seek a position in the public relations field—a tough one to break into for anyone! As an educator, you gained some *"extracurricular"* experience in some public-relations type activities (served as the school's liaison with the PTA' coordinated fund-raising projects for senior plays; wrote and delivered speeches at student events; chaired district-wide committee which developed, designed, and printed new *"PR"* brochure for school system). In addition, you joined Toastmasters International, progressed steadily through their public speaking program, served as a club officer and recently were elected as a district representative. Furthermore, you chair your church's membership committee, recruit and welcome new members, and get them involved with church life. When you reviewed your achievements, the public relations theme was obvious. Consequently, you decided to explore PR opportunities.

Your interests and related background information can be presented in a positive manner during the interview. This positive strategy is evident in the following interview dialogue:

QUESTION: **"Isn't conference promotion and coordination a major change for you?"** (concern: purpose, demonstrated interest, abilities)

YOU: *"On the surface, it may appear like an abrupt change for me, but, in reality, it's a natural development from* *my career interests. For the past seven years, I have been involved in public relations-type activities both within and outside education, and I've found that I not only enjoy the work but seem to have a flair for it. For example, I chaired a district-wide committee which developed a new public relations piece when staff were still being recruited. I was involved in every aspect of the project—conceptualization, design, writing copy, layout, photography, and publication. It is still being used today. In addition, I supervised several fundraising projects through which I worked with local businesses, the media, parents, students, and the school administration. Those required a lot of selling and promotion. I've written and given numerous speeches in several settings and I have leadership experience at the local and district levels with Toastmasters International, where I've planned and conducted programs. Furthermore, I've coordinated successful membership drives, welcomed newcomers and got them involved with activities to keep up their interest.*

So, when I examined those activities which I enjoyed doing and did well, public relations-type work seemed like a natural choice. Over the years, I learned how to coordinate people and events, present ideas and activities in a way which projects a positive image, and gets people interested and involved in events. I enjoy the challenge of being involved with a project from beginning to end, working with different people, groups and organizations, promoting events, and meeting deadlines. In addition, I'm very familiar with our city, its attractions and its organizations. Through Toastmasters and other activities, I've met key business and civic leaders and know how to involve others in a project."

QUESTION: **"What appeals to you about our position as conference coordinator?"** (concern: enthusiasm for job, demonstrated interest)

YOU: *"Well, there are a number of things. First, your*
              requirements call for skills and experience which I
              have—ability to promote ideas and events; organize
              and involve people; handle all aspects of publicity;
              work with the media, advertising agencies, businesses,
              and municipal officials; meet deadlines; work without
              close supervision; take initiative and solve problems.
              Second, the position is very much in line with my
              career interests, and because of related past ex-
              perience, I know that I'd enjoy doing the work. It seems
              like a good match from my perspective. Third, I like
              what I see here. The staff seems enthusiastic, friendly,
              and hard working. The plans you have for developing
              new business are exciting, especially the project to
              coordinate conference events with the tourist bureau
              and the Chamber of Commerce."

The most difficult challenge to your positive strategy comes when the
interviewer asks you to describe your negatives or weaknesses:

**QUESTION: "We all have our negatives and weaknesses. What
are some of yours?'**

You can handle this question in five different ways, yet still give positive
information on yourself:

1. **Discuss a negative which is not related in anyway to the
    job under consideration:**

    "Well, to be honest about it, I've never particularly enjoyed
    repetitive tasks which are quantitative in nature. Perhaps that's
    one reason I've enjoyed my work and PR activities so much;
    they require very little in the way of math. Now, that's not to
    say that I can't perform quantitative tasks. For example, I think
    I do a good job in managing the family budget and deal real
    well in maintaining the financial records for Toastmasters. But
    neither one was my peak experience, if you know what I
    mean?"

2. Discuss a negative which the Interviewer already knows:

"As you see from my resume, most of my paid experience is in education. Although I've had considerable PR experience, I'm afraid that my job title as "teacher" will cause potential employers to stereotype me as another one of those educators who is reacting to problems in education and to not take a closer look at me as an individual. However, my exploration of career options is not simply a reaction to the situation in education. It is a result of a lot of soul searching and hard evaluation. When I carefully and honestly assess what I enjoy doing and do well, my public relations activities stand out from all the rest."

3. Discuss a negative which you have improved upon:

"Well, like a lot of people, I sometimes get a little too wrapped up in my work, to the point of neglecting personal things. For example, with teaching, Toastmasters, and some other commitments, I found myself working all day, then running off to meetings several evenings per week. With these commitments plus my family obligations, there wasn't much time left for me and I gave my physical fitness low priority for awhile. However, I recognized that, in responding to all these demands, my life got a little out of balance. So, what I did was assess priorities and adjust my schedule to allow some time for me. Consequently, I've put myself on a regular exercise program—3 days per week—and feel like I've achieved that nice balance again. Besides, I feel better, have much more energy, and seem to actually be able to work more efficiently than before."

4. Discuss a *"negative"* which can also be a positive:

"I guess I'd have to say that I can become annoyed by certain types of people. You know...there are several teachers I work with who are always complaining about this, that, and the other thing. Nothing is ever right in their eyes. They're always complaining and negative, especially when others present new ideas or try to make improvements. Yet, they don't want to act or follow through on any of their complaints. You know the type—'Let Joe do it. It's not my responsibility.' Then they

criticize Joe for trying. Well, I've always believed that if anything positive is going to happen, a person needs to assume some responsibility and make a contribution, however small. If we all waited around for 'Joe to do it', nothing would ever get done."

5. Discuss a negative outside yourself:

"I don't feel that there is anything seriously wrong with me. Like most people, I have my ups and downs—that's normal—but overall I have a positive outlook, feel good about myself and what I've accomplished so far in my life. However, I am somewhat concerned how you might view my wanting to change occupations. I want to assure you that I'm not making this change on a whim. I've taken my time in thinking through the issues and taking a hard look at what I do well and enjoy doing. If anything, this change is a fine tuning of my career direction. Like a lot of young people, I guess I didn't have much life experience when I started my career ten years ago, and I got into teaching because I enjoyed that kind of environment. However, as I got more experience and had opportunities to become involved in different areas, my interest in PR developed and I found that I not only enjoyed those activities, but that I had some natural talent for them. While I've enjoyed my years in education, I am committed to finding work more in line with my interests and abilities."

All of these examples stress the basic point about effective interviewing. Your single best strategy for managing the interview is to emphasize your strengths and positives. Questions come in several forms. Practice with these questions, especially the negative ones, in order to best control your interview situation.

ILLEGAL QUESTIONS

Other questions are illegal, but some employers ask them nonetheless. Consider how you would respond to questions interviewers should not be asking:

• *Are you married, divorced, separated, or single?*

- *How old are you?*
- *Do you go to church regularly?*
- *Do you have many debts?*
- *Do you own or rent your home?*
- *What social and political organizations do you belong to?*
- *What does your spouse think about your career?*
- *Are you living with anyone?*
- *Are you practicing birth control?*
- *Were you ever arrested?*
- *How much insurance do you have?*
- *How much do you weigh?*
- *How tall are you?*

Don't get upset and say *"That's an illegal question...I refuse to answer it!"* While you may be perfectly right in saying so, this response lacks tact, which may be what the employer is looking for. For example, if you are divorced and the interviewer asks about your divorce, you might respond with *"Does a divorce have a direct bearing on the responsibilities of this position?"* Some employers may ask such questions just to see how you answer or react under stress. Others may do so out of ignorance of the law.

ASKING QUESTIONS

Interviewers expect candidates to ask intelligent questions concerning the organization and the nature of the work. Moreover, you need information and should indicate your interest in the employer by asking questions. Consider asking some of these questions if they haven't been answered early in the interview:

- *Tell me about the duties and responsibilities of this job.*
- *How does this position relate to other positions within this organization?*
- *How long has this position been in the organization?*
- *What would be the ideal type of person for this position? Skills? Personality? Working style? Background?*
- *Can you tell me about the people who have been in this position before? Backgrounds? Promotions? Terminations?*
- *Whom would I be working with in this position?*

- *Tell me something about these people? Strengths? Weaknesses? Performance expectations?*
- *What am I expected to accomplish during the first year?*
- *How will I be evaluated?*
- *Are promotions and raises tied to performance criteria?*
- *Tell me how this operates?*
- *What is the normal salary range for such a position?*
- *Based on your experience, what type of problems would someone new in this position likely encounter?*
- *I'm interested in your career with this organization. When did you start? What are your plans for the future?*
- *I would like to know how people get promoted and advance in this organization?*
- *What is particularly unique about working in this organization?*
- *Can you explain the various benefits employees receive?*
- *What does the future look like for this organization?*

You may want to write your questions on a 3 x 5 card and take them with you to the interview. While it is best to memorize these questions, you may need to refer to your list when the interviewer asks you if you have any questions. You might do this by saying: *"Yes, I jotted down a few questions which I want to make sure I ask you before leaving."* Then pull out your card and refer to the questions.

DRESS APPROPRIATELY

Appearance is the first thing you communicate to others. Before you have a chance to speak, others notice how you dress and accordingly draw certain conclusions about your personality and competence. Indeed, research shows that appearance makes the greatest difference when an evaluator has little information about the other person. This is precisely the situation you find yourself in at the start of the interview.

Many people object to having their capabilities evaluated on the basis of their appearance and manner of dress. *"But that is not fair,"* they argue. *"People should be hired on the basis of their ability to do the job—not on how they look."* But debating the lack of merit or complaining about the unfairness of such behavior does not alter reality. Like it or not, people do make initial judgments about others based on their appearance. Since you cannot alter this fact and bemoaning it will get you nowhere, it is best to learn to use it to your advantage. If you learn to effectively manage your image, you can convey marvelous messages regarding your authority, credibility, and competence.

Some estimates indicate that as much as 65 percent of the hiring decision may be based on the nonverbal aspects of the interview! Employers sometimes refer to this phenomenon with such terms as *"chemistry"*, *"body warmth"*, or that *"gut feeling"* the individual is right for the job. This correlates with findings of communication studies that approximately 65 percent of a message is communicated nonverbally. The remaining 35 percent is communicated verbally.

Rules of the Game

Knowing how to dress appropriately for the interview requires knowing important rules of the game. Like it or not, employers play by these rules. Once you know the rules, you at least can make a conscious choice whether or not you want to play. If you decide to play, you will stand a better chance of winning by using the often unwritten rules to your advantage.

Much has been written on how to dress professionally, especially since John Molloy first wrote his books on dress for success in the 1970s. While this approach has been criticized for promoting a *"cookie cutter"* or *"carbon copy"* image, it is still valid for most interview situations. The degree to which employers adhere to these rules, however, will depend on particular individuals and situations. Your job is to know when, where, and to what extent the rules apply to you. When in doubt, follow our general advice on looking professional.

Knowing and playing by the rules does not imply incompetent people get jobs simply by dressing the part. Rather, it implies that qualified and competent job applicants can gain an extra edge over a field of other qualified, competent individuals by dressing to convey positive professional images.

Winning the Game

Much advice has been written about how to dress for success—some of it excellent. However, there is a major flaw in most of the advice you encounter. Researchers on the subject have looked at how people in positions of power view certain colors for professional attire. Few have gone beyond this to note that colors do different things on different people. Various shades or clarities of a color or combinations of contrast between light and dark colors when worn together may be unenhancing to some individuals and actually diminish that person's "power look".

If you combine the results of research done by John Molloy on how colors relate to one's power look and that done by JoAnne Nicholson and Judy Lewis-Crum as explained in their book *Color Wonderful* (New York: Bantam) on how colors relate to us as unique individuals, you can achieve a win-win situation. You can retain your individuality and look your most enhanced while, at the same time, achieving a look of success, power, and competence.

Your Winning Appearance

The key to effective dressing is to know how to relate the clothing you put on your body to your own natural coloring. Into which category does your coloring fit? Let's find out where you belong in terms of color type:

- **Contrast coloring:** If you are a contrast color type, you have a definite dark-light appearance. You have very dark brown or black hair and light to medium ivory or olive toned skin. Black men and women in this category will have clear light to dark skin tones and dark hair.

- **Light-bright coloring:** If you are of this color type, you have golden tones in your skin and golden tones in your blond or light to medium brown hair. Most of you had blond or light brown hair as children. Black men and women in this category will have clear golden skin in their face and dark hair.

- **Muted coloring:** If you are a muted color type, you have a definite brown-on-brown or red-on- brown appearance. Your skin tone is an ivory-beige, brown-beige, or golden-beige tone— that is, you have a beige skin with a golden-brown cast. Your hair could be red or light to dark brown with camel, bronze, or red highlights. Black men and women in this category will have golden or brown skin tones and dark hair.

- **Gentle coloring:** If you are of this color type, you have a soft, gentle looking appearance. Your skintone is a light ivory or pink-beige tone and your hair is ash blond or ash brown. You probably had blond or ash brown hair as a child. Black men and women in this category will have pink tones in their skin and dark hair.

There are also some individuals who may be a combination of two color types. If your skin tone falls in one category and your hair color in another, you are a combination color type.

However, if you are not certain which hair or skin tone is yours and are hence undecided as to which color type category you belong to, you may wish to contact Color 1 Associates at 1/800-523-8496 (2211 Washington Circle, NW, Washington, DC 20037). In addition, the *Color Wonderful* book includes a listing of professionally trained associates located nearest you.

Color 1 can provide you with an individualized color chart that allows you to wear every color in the spectrum, but in your best *shade* and *clarity* as well as written material telling you how you can combine your colors for the best amounts of contrast for your natural coloring (color type).

The color chart is an excellent one-time investment considering the costs of buying the wrong colored suit, shirt, or blouse. It will more than pay for itself if it contributes to an effective interview as you wear your suit in your best shade and put your clothing together to work with, rather than against, your natural coloring. It can help you convey positive images during those crucial initial minutes of the interview—as well as over a lifetime.

Images of Success

John Molloy has conducted extensive research on how individuals can dress effectively. Aimed at individuals already working in professional positions who want to communicate a success image, his advice is just as relevant for someone interviewing for a job.

Basic attire for men or women interviewing for a position is a suit. Let's look at appropriate suits in terms of color, fabric, and style. The suit color can make a difference in creating an image of authority and competence. The suit colors that make the strongest positive statements for you are *your shade* of gray in a medium to charcoal depth or *your shade* of blue in a medium to navy depth of color. However, you may choose a less authoritative look for some interview settings. Camel or beige are also considered proper colors for men's suits and women have an even greater color range. Generally even women should select fairly conservative colors for a job interview unless you are interviewing for a job in a field where non-conformity is considered a plus.

When selecting your suit, choose a shade that is enhancing to you. Should you wear a blue-gray, a taupe-gray, or a shade in-between? Do you look better in a somewhat bright navy or a more toned-down navy; a blue navy or a black navy; a navy with a purple or a yellow base to it?

In general, most people will look better in somewhat blue grays than in grays that are closer to the taupe side of the spectrum. Most people will be enhanced by a navy that is not too bright or contain so much black that it is difficult to distinguish whether the color is navy or black. When selecting a beige or a camel, select a tone that complements your skin color. If your skin has pink tones, avoid beiges and camels that contain gold hues and select pink based beiges/camels that enhance your skin color. Similarly, those of you who have gold/olive tones to your skin should avoid the pink based camel and beiges.

Your suit(s) should be made of a natural fiber. A good blend of a natural fiber with some synthetic is acceptable as long as it has the *"look"* of the natural fiber. The very best suit fabrics are wool, wool blends, or fabrics that look like them. Even for the warmer summer months, men can find summer weight wool suits that are comfortable and look marvelous. They are your best buy. For really hot climates, a linen/silk fabric can work well. Normally a linen will have to be blended with another fiber, often a synthetic, in order to retain a pressed, neat look. The major disadvantage of pure linen is that it wrinkles. Women's suits also should be made of a natural fiber or have the *"look"* of a natural fiber. The very best winter-weight suit fabrics are wool or wool blends. For the warmer climates or the summer months, women will find few, if any, summer weight wool suits made for them. Hence linen, blended with a synthetic so it will not look as if it needs constant pressing or a good silk or silk blend are good choices. Avoid 100 percent polyester materials, or anything that looks like it—especially double-knits— like the plague! It is a definite negative for your look of competence, power, and success.

The style of your suit should be classic. It should be well-tailored and well-styled. Avoid suits that appear *"trendy"* unless you are applying for a job in a field such as arts or perhaps advertising. A conservative suit that has a timeless classic styling and also looks up-to-date will serve you best not only for the interview, but it will give you several years wear once you land the job.

Men should select a shirt color that is lighter than the color of their suit. John Molloy's book on appearance and dress for men, **Dress For Success**, goes into great detail on shirts, ties, and practically everything you might wear or carry with you. We recommend Molloy's book over others because it is based on research rather than personal opinion and promotional fads.

When deciding on your professional wardrobe, always buy clothes to last and buy quality.

When deciding on your professional wardrobe, always buy clothes to last and buy quality. For women quality means buying silk blouses if you can afford them. Keep in mind not only the price of the blouse itself, but the cleaning bill. There are many polyester blouse fabrics that have the look and feel of silk—this is an exception to the *"no polyester"* rule. Silk or a polyester that has the look and feel of silk are the fabrics for blouses to go with your suits. Choose your blouses in your most flattering shades and clarity of color. John Molloy's book on appearance and dress for women, **The Woman's Dress for Success Book**, goes into great detail on the blouse styles that test best as well as expands on suit colors. It includes information on almost anything you might wear or carry with you to the interview or on the job.

Give your outfit a more *"finished and polished"* look by accessorizing it effectively. Collect silk scarves and necklaces of semiprecious stones in your suit colors. Wear scarves and necklaces with your suits and blouses in such a way that they repeat the color of the suit. For example, a woman wearing a navy suit and a red silk blouse could accent the look by wearing a necklace of navy sodalite beads or a silk scarf that has navy as a predominate color. The **Color Wonderful** book includes a great deal of information to help you accessorize your look geared to your color type.

APPEAR LIKEABLE

Remember, most people invited to a job interview have already been *"screened in"*. They supposedly possess the basic qualifications for the job, such as education and work experience. At this point employers will look for several qualities in the candidates, such as honesty, credibility, intelligence, competence, enthusiasm, spontaneity, friendliness, and likeability. Much of the message communicating these qualities will be conveyed through your dress as well as through other nonverbal behaviors.

In the end, employers hire people they *like* and who will interact well on an interpersonal basis with the rest of the staff. Therefore, you should communicate that you are a likeable candidate who can get along well with others. You can communicate these messages by engaging in several nonverbal behaviors. Four of the most important ones include:

1. **Sit with a very slight forward lean toward the interviewer.** It should be so slight as to be almost imperceptible. If not overdone and obvious, it communicates your interest in what the interviewer is saying.

2. **Make eye contact frequently, but don't overdo it.** Good eye contact establishes rapport with the interviewer. You will be perceived as more trustworthy if you will look at the interviewer as you ask and answer questions. To say someone has *"shifty eyes"* or cannot *"look us in the eye"* is to imply they may not be completely honest. To have a direct, though moderate eye gaze, conveys interest, as well as trustworthiness.

3. **A moderate amount of smiling will also help reinforce your positive image.** You should smile enough to convey your positive attitude, but not so much that you will not be taken seriously. Some people naturally smile often and others hardly ever smile. Monitor your behavior or ask a friend to give you honest feedback.

4. **Try to convey interest and enthusiasm through your vocal inflections.** Your tone of voice can say a lot about you and how interested you are in the interviewer and organization.

CLOSE THE INTERVIEW

Be prepared to end the interview. Many people don't know when or how to close interviews. They go on and on until someone breaks an uneasy moment of silence with an indication that it is time to go.

Interviewers normally will initiate the close by standing, shaking hands, and thanking you for coming to the interview. Don't end by saying *"Goodbye and thank you"*. As this stage, you should summarize the interview in terms of your interests, strengths, and goals. Briefly restate your qualifications and continuing interest in working with the employer. At this point it is proper to ask the interviewer about selection plans: *"When do you anticipate making your final decision?"* Follow this question with your final one: *"May I call you next week to inquire about my status?"* By taking the initiative in this manner, the employer will be prompted to clarify your status soon, and you will have an opportunity to talk to her further.

Many interviewers will ask you for a list of references. Be sure to prepare such a list prior to the interview. Include the names, addresses, and phone numbers of four individuals who will give you positive professional and personal recommendations.

REMEMBER TO FOLLOW-UP

Once you have been interviewed, be sure to follow through to get nearer to the job offer. One of the best follow-up methods is the thank-you letter. After talking to the employer over the telephone or in a face-to-face interview, send a thank-you letter. This letter should be typed on good quality bond paper. In this letter express your gratitude for the opportunity to interview. Re-state your interest in the position and highlight any particularly noteworthy points made in your conversation or anything you wish to further clarify. Close the letter by mentioning that you will call in a few days to inquire about the employer's decision. When you do this, the employer should remember you as a thoughtful person.

If you call and the employer has not yet made a decision, follow through with another phone call in a few days. Send any additional information to the employer which may enhance your application. You might also want to ask one of your references to call the employer to further recommend you for the position. However, don't engage in overkill by making a pest of yourself. You want to tactfully communicate two things to the employer at this point: (1) you are interested in the job, and (2) you will do a good job.

For more information on developing interviewing skills, look for the Krannichs' *Interview For Success.* If you wish greater depth on negotiating salary than what you find here, you may wish to consult the Krannichs' *Salary Success.*

NEGOTIATE THE BEST SALARY

Salary is one of the most important yet least understood considerations in the job search. Many individuals do well in handling all interview questions except the salary question. They are either too shy to talk about money or they believe you must take what you are offered because salary is predetermined by employers. Many teachers have little experience in negotiating salaries since their past salaries were largely predetermined by school boards or deans and thus know little about dealing with money questions. As a result, many applicants may be paid much less than they are worth. Over the years, they will lose thousands of dollars by having failed to properly negotiate their salaries.

Many applicants are paid much less than they are worth.

Since most salaries outside education are negotiable, the salary question may arise at any time. Employers like to raise the question as soon as possible in order to screen candidates in or out. You, on the other hand, want to deal with the salary question toward the end—after you learn more about the job and demonstrate your value to the employer. Your goal should be to get a job interview and job offer as well as negotiate as high a salary as possible.

Strategies

A standard salary negotiation scenario is for the employer to raise this question: "What are your salary requirements?" When faced with this question, you should turn it around by asking the employer: *"What is the normal range in your organization for a position such as this as well as for someone with my qualifications?"* The employer will either try again to get you to state a figure by restating the original question or reveal the actual range. Expect a frank answer most of the time. If the employer indicates a range, the rest of the salary negotiation is relatively simple.

Having done your homework on salaries and knowing what you are worth and what the employer is willing to pay, you are now ready to do some friendly but earnest haggling. If, for example, the employer says his range for the position is $40,000 to $45,000, you might respond by saying *"$45,000 is within my range".* If his range is much more or less than you anticipated, avoid being emotional or overly positive or negative. Disregard the bottom figure and concentrate on working from the top by putting his highest figure into the bottom of your range. For example, if he says *"$40,000 to $45,000",* you should move the top figure into your $45,000 to $50,000 range. By doing this, you create common ground from which to negotiate or you neutralize the salary issue until later negotiations.

However, if the employer does not state a range or states only a single figure, such as $40,000, rely on your salary research or multiply this figure by 25 percent to arrive at a figure for negotiation. Thus, the $40,000 figure now becomes your $48,000 expectation. Respond by saying, *"I'm thinking more in terms of $48,000".* A $8,000 difference should give you room for negotiation. If you state $60,000, you may appear unreasonable, unless you can support this figure based upon your salary research on comparable positions. But your previous salary research should result in stating a reasonable salary range which can be documented for similar positions in this or other organizations.

Employers may praise their *"benefits"* package prior to talking about a cash figure. Be wary of such benefits. Most are standard and thus come with the job regardless of the salary figure you negotiate. Unless you can create some special benefits, such as an extra two weeks of paid vacation each year, you should focus your attention primarily on the base salary figure.

Raise the Base

The salary figure you negotiate will influence subsequent salaries with this and other organizations. In fact, many employers figure your present worth based on your salary history; they simply add 10 to 15 percent to what you made in your last job to arrive at your new salary. If you were an

$25,000 a year teacher, such a procedure will discriminate against you and your talents. Since as a teacher you were working at a depressed salary, you may have difficulty justifying a major salary increase in the eyes of most employers. In this case, you need to change the rules of game. Disregard your salary history and, instead, focus on both your worth and the value of the position to the employer—not on what the employer can get you for. On the other hand, if you are coming from a $60,000 a year job to a $45,000 one, you must convince the employer that you will be happy with a salary decrease—if, indeed, you can live with it. Many employers will not expect you to remain long if you take such a salary cut; thus, they may be reluctant to offer you a position.

Renegotiate

You should make sure your future salary reflects your value. One approach to doing this is to reach an agreement to renegotiate your salary at a later date, perhaps in another six to eight months. Use this technique especially when you feel the final salary offer is less than what you are worth, but you want to accept the job. Employers often will agree to this provision since they have nothing to lose and much to gain if you are as productive as you tell them.

However, be prepared to renegotiate in both directions—up and down. If the employer does not want to give you the salary figure you want, you can create good will by proposing to negotiate the higher salary figure down after six months, if your performance does not meet the employer's expectations. On the other hand, you may accept his lower figure with the provision that the two of you will negotiate your salary up after six months, if you exceed the employer's expectations. It is preferable to start out high and negotiate down rather than start low and negotiate up.

Renegotiation provisions stress one very important point: you want to be paid on the basis of your performance. You demonstrate your professionalism, self-confidence, and competence by negotiating in this manner. More important, you ensure that the question of your monetary value will not be closed in the future. As you negotiate the present, you also negotiate your future with this as well as other employers.

Reach Agreement

You should accept an offer only after reaching a salary agreement. If you jump at an offer, you may appear needy. Take time to consider your options. Remember, you are committing your time and effort in exchange for money and status. Is this the job you really want? Take some time to think about the offer before giving the employer a definite answer. But don't play hard-to-get and thereby create ill-will with your new employer. How you interview and negotiate your salary will influence how well you get along with your employer on the job.

While considering the offer, ask yourself several of the same questions you asked at the beginning of your job search:

- *What do I want to be doing five years from now?*
- *How will this job affect my personal life?*
- *Do I want to travel?*
- *Do I know enough about the employer and the future of this organization?*
- *Are there other jobs I'm considering which would better meet my goals?*

Accepting a job is serious business. If you make a mistake, you could be locked into a very unhappy situation for a long time.

If you receive one job offer while considering another, you will be able to compare relative advantages and disadvantages. You also will have some external leverage for negotiating salary and benefits. While you should not play games, let the employer know you have alternative job offers. This communicates that you are in demand, others also know your value, and the employer's price is not the only one in town. Use this leverage to negotiate your salary, benefits, and job responsibilities.

If you get a job offer but you are considering other employers, let the others know you have a job offer. Telephone them to inquire about your status as well as inform them of the job offer. Sometimes this will prompt employers to make a hiring decision sooner than anticipated. In addition, you will be informing them that you are in demand; they should seriously consider you before you get away!

Some job seekers play a bluffing game by telling employers they have alternative job offers even though they don't. Some candidates do this and get away with it. We don't recommend this approach. Not only is it dishonest, it will work to your disadvantage if the employer learns that you were lying. But more important, you should be selling yourself on the basis of your strengths rather than your cleverness and greed. If you can't sell yourself by being honest, don't expect to get along well on the job. When you compromise your integrity, you demean your value to others and yourself.

Your job search is not over with the job offer and acceptance. One final word of advice. Be thoughtful by sending your new employer a nice thank-you letter. This is one of the most effective letters to write for getting your new job off on the right foot. The employer will remember you as a thoughtful individual whom he looks forward to working with.

The whole point of these job search methods is to clearly communicate to employers that you are competent and worthy of being paid top dollar. If you follow this advice, you should do very well with employers in interviews and in negotiating your salary as well as working on a new job outside education!

Chapter Thirteen

TURN YOUR
GOALS INTO REALITIES

Understanding without action is a waste of time. And buying a how-to book without implementing it is a waste of money. Many people read how-to books, attend how-to seminars, and do nothing other than read more books, attend more seminars, and engage in more wishful thinking. While these activities become forms of therapy for some individuals, they should lead to positive actions for you.

From the very beginning of this book we stressed the importance of developing appropriate job search strategies for finding jobs outside education. We make no assumptions nor claim any magic is contained in this book. Rather, we have attempted to assemble useful information to help you organize an effective job search which will best communicate your qualifications to potential employers. Individual chapters examined job market myths, trends, and specific job search skills such as writing resumes and conducting informational interviews. We have done our part in getting you to the implementation stage. What happens next is your responsibility.

Assuming you have a firm understanding of each job search step and how to relate them to your goals, what do you do next? The next steps involve **hard work**. Just how motivated are you to seek a new career outside education? Our experience is that individuals need to be sufficiently **motivated** to make the first move and do it properly. If you go about your job search half-heartedly—you just want to *"test the waters outside education"*—to see what's out there—don't expect to be successful. You must be committed to achieving specific goals. Make the decision to properly develop and implement your job search and be prepared to work hard in achieving your goals.

Understanding without action is a waste of time. And buying a how-to book without implementing it is a waste of money.

Once you've convinced yourself to take the necessary steps to find a job outside education, you need to find the *time* to properly implement your job search. This requires setting aside specific blocks of time for identifying your motivated abilities and skills, developing your resume, writing letters, making telephone calls, and conducting the necessary research and networking required for success. This whole process takes time. If you are a busy person, like most people, you simply must make the time. Practice your own versions of time management or cutback management. Get better organized, give some things up, or cut back on all your activities. If, for example, you can set aside one hour each day to devote to your job search, you will spend seven hours a week or 28 hours a month on your search. However, you should and can find more time than this for these activities.

Time and again we find successful job hunters are ones who routinize a job search schedule and keep at it. They make contact after contact, conduct numerous informational interviews, submit many applications and resumes, and keep repeating these activities in spite of encountering rejections. They learn that success is just a few more *"nos"* and information- al interviews away!

You may find it useful to commit yourself in writing to achieving job search success. This is a very useful way to get both motivated and directed for action. Start by completing the following job search contract and keep it near you—in your briefcase or on your desk.

JOB SEARCH CONTRACT

1. I will begin my job search on _____.
2. I will involve <u>(individual/group)</u> with my job search.
3. I will complete my skills identification step by ___.
4. I will complete my objective statement by ____.
5. I will complete my resume by ____.
6. Each week I will:
   - make ____ new job contacts.
   - conduct ____ informational interviews.
   - follow-up on ____ referrals.
7. My first job interview will take place during the week of ____.
8. I will begin my new job on ____.
9. I will manage my time so that I can successfully complete my job search and find a high quality job.

Signature: _____

Date: _____

In addition, you should complete weekly performance reports. These reports identify what you actually accomplished rather than what your good intentions tell you to do. Make copies of the following performance and planning report form and use one each week to track your actual progress and to plan your activities for the next week.

WEEKLY JOB SEARCH PERFORMANCE AND PLANNING REPORT

1. The week of: _____.
2. This week I:
   - wrote ___ job search letters.
   - sent ___ resumes and ___ letters to potential employers.
   - completed ___ applications.
   - made ___ job search telephone calls.
   - completed ___ hours of job research.

- set up ___ appointments for informational interviews.
- conducted ___ informational interviews.
- received ___ invitations to a job interview.
- followed up on ___ contacts and ___ referrals.

3. Next week I will:
   - write ___ job search letters.
   - send ___ resumes and ___ letters to potential employers.
   - complete ___ applications.
   - make ___ job search telephone calls.
   - complete ___ hours of job research.
   - set up ___ appointments for informational interviews.
   - conduct ___ informational interviews.
   - follow up on ___ contacts and ___ referrals.

4. Summary of progress this week in reference to my Job Search Contract commitments:

   _____
   _____
   _____
   _____

If you fail to meet these written commitments, issue yourself a revised and updated contract. But if you do this three or more times, we strongly suggest you stop kidding yourself about your motivation and commitment to find a job outside education. Start over again, but this time consult a professional career counselor who can provide you with the necessary structure to make progress in finding a job.

A professional may not be cheap, but if paying for help gets you on the right track and results in the job you want, it's money well spent. Do not be *"penny wise but pound foolish"* with your future. If you must seek professional advice, be sure you are an informed consumer according to our *"shopping"* advice in Chapter Four.

Careers and jobs should not be viewed as life sentences. You should feel free to change jobs and careers whenever you want to. In fact, thousands of educators make successful career transitions each year. Some are more successful than others in finding the right job. If you plan your career transition according to the methods outlined in previous chapters, you should be able to successfully land the job you want. Above all, take the time to sail into today's job market with a plan of action that links your qualifications to the needs of employers. While you may have an occupational background in the field of education, you are first and foremost an individual with knowledge, abilities, and skills that many employers need and want. If you follow the advice of this book, you will put your best foot forward in communicating your qualifications to employers.

INDEX

CAREER RESOURCES

Call or write IMPACT PUBLICATIONS to receive a free copy of their latest comprehensive, illustrated, and annotated catalog of over 1,000 career resources.

The following career resources are available directly from Impact Publications. Complete the following form or list the titles, include postage (see formula at the end), enclose payment, and send your order to:

IMPACT PUBLICATIONS
4580 Sunshine Court
Woodbridge, VA 22192
Tel. 703/361-7300
FAX 703/335-9486

Orders from individuals must be prepaid by check, moneyorder, Visa or MasterCard number. We accept telephone and FAX orders with a Visa or MasterCard number.

Qty.	TITLES	Price	TOTAL

EDUCATORS

____	Academic Job Digest	$29.95	____
____	Alternative Careers for Teachers	$8.95	____
____	Careers in Education	$16.95	____
____	Educator's Guide to Alternative Jobs and Careers	$13.95	____
____	Teachers in New Careers	$14.95	____

CAREER CHANGES

____	Careering and Re-Careering For the 1990s	$12.95	____
____	From Campus to Corporation	$10.95	____
____	Graduating to the 9-5 World	$12.95	____

____ Starting Over $11.95 ____
____ Transitions $10.95 ____

JOB SEARCH STRATEGIES AND TACTICS

____ Complete Job Search Handbook $12.95 ____
____ Go Hire Yourself an Employer $9.95 ____
____ Joyce Lane Kennedy's Career Book $29.95 ____
____ The Right Place at the Right Time $11.95 ____
____ Super Job Search $24.95 ____
____ Wishcraft $7.95 ____
____ Who's Hiring Who $10.95 ____

SKILLS IDENTIFICATION, TESTING, AND SELF-ASSESSMENT

____ Career Sort Assessment Instruments $23.95 ____
____ CareerMap $12.95 ____
____ Charting Your Goals $12.95 ____
____ Discover the Right Job For You! $11.95 ____
____ Discover What You're Best At $10.95 ____
____ Quick Job Hunting Map $3.95 ____
____ The Real-Life Aptitude Test $10.95 ____
____ The Three Boxes of Life $14.95 ____
____ The Truth About You $11.95 ____
____ What Color Is Your Parachute? $11.95 ____
____ Where Do I Go From Here With My Life? $11.95 ____

RESEARCH ON JOBS, ORGANIZATIONS, CITIES, AND FIELDS

____ 101 Careers $12.95 ____
____ American Almanac of Jobs and Salaries $15.95 ____
____ America's Phone Book $24.95 ____
____ California $9.95 ____
____ Career Finder $14.95 ____
____ Careers Encyclopedia $29.95 ____
____ Dictionary of Occupational Titles $32.95 ____
____ Directory of Executive Recruiters (1991) $39.95 ____
____ Encyclopedia of Careers & Vocational Guidance   129.95 ____
____ Exploring Careers $19.95 ____
____ Great Careers $36.95 ____
____ Guide to Occupational Exploration $36.95 ____
____ *"How to Be Happily Employed In..."* Boston, Dallas/
     Ft. Worth, San Francisco, Washington, DC ($10.95
     each or $42.95 for set of 4) $42.95 ____
____ *"How to Get a Job In..."* Atlanta, Chicago, Dallas/
     Ft. Worth, Houston, Los Angeles/San Diego, New
     York, San Francisco, Seattle/Portland, Washington,
     DC ($15.95 each or $139.95 for set of 9) $139.95 ____

_____ **Job Bank Series:** Atlanta, Boston, Chicago, Dallas,
Denver, Detroit, Florida, Houston, Los Angeles,
Minneapolis, New York, Ohio, Philadelphia, San
Francisco, Seattle, St. Louis, Washington, DC
($12.95 each or $219.95 for set of 17)	$219.95 _____
_____ Jobs! What They Are, Where They Are...	$11.95 _____
_____ Jobs 1991	$14.95 _____
_____ Jobs Rated Almanac	$14.95 _____
_____ L.A. Job Market Handbook	$15.95 _____
_____ National Trade and Professional Associations	$59.95 _____
_____ Occupational Outlook Handbook	$22.95 _____
_____ Places Rated Almanac	$16.95 _____
_____ Top Professionals	$10.95 _____

RESUMES, LETTERS, AND NETWORKING

_____ 200 Letters for Job Hunters	$14.95 _____
_____ Damn Good Resume Guide	$7.95 _____
_____ Does Your Resume Wear Apron Strings?	$7.95 _____
_____ Does Your Resume Wear Blue Jeans?	$7.95 _____
_____ Dynamite Cover Letters	$9.95 _____
_____ Dynamite Resumes	$9.95 _____
_____ Great Connections	$11.95 _____
_____ High Impact Resumes and Letters	$12.95 _____
_____ Is Your "Net" Working?	$22.95 _____
_____ Network Your Way to Job and Career Success	$11.95 _____
_____ Perfect Cover Letter	$9.95 _____
_____ Perfect Resume	$10.95 _____
_____ Resume Catalog	$13.95 _____
_____ Resumes That Knock 'Em Dead	$7.95 _____
_____ Sure-Hire Resumes	$14.95 _____
_____ Your First Resume	$10.95 _____

DRESS, APPEARANCE, AND IMAGE

_____ Color Me Beautiful	$17.95 _____
_____ Dress for Success	$9.95 _____
_____ Dressing Smart	$19.95 _____
_____ Professional Image	$10.95 _____
_____ New Etiquette	$14.95 _____
_____ Secret Language of Success	$18.95 _____
_____ Women's Dress for Success	$8.95 _____
_____ Working Wardrobe	$11.95 _____

INTERVIEWS AND SALARY NEGOTIATIONS

_____ Five Minute Interview	$12.95 _____
_____ How to Get Interviews From Job Ads	$16.95 _____
_____ How to Make $1,000 a Minute	$7.95 _____

____ Interview for Success $11.95 ____
____ Power Interviews $12.95 ____
____ Salary Success $11.95 ____
____ Sweaty Palms $8.95 ____

PUBLIC-ORIENTED CAREERS

____ 171 Reference Book $18.95 ____
____ American Almanac of Government Jobs and Careers $14.95 ____
____ Compleat Guide to Finding Jobs in Government $14.95 ____
____ Complete Guide to Public Employment $15.95 ____
____ Find a Federal Job Fast! $9.95 ____
____ Getting Started in Federal Contracting $21.95 ____
____ How to Get a Federal Job $15.00 ____
____ Profitable Careers in Nonprofit $12.95 ____
____ SF-171 Express

INTERNATIONAL AND OVERSEAS JOBS

____ Almanac of International Jobs and Careers $14.95 ____
____ Complete Guide to International Jobs and Careers $13.95 ____
____ Guide to Careers in World Affairs $11.95 ____
____ How to Get a Job in Europe $15.95 ____
____ International Careers $11.95 ____
____ International Consultant $22.95 ____
____ International Jobs $12.95 ____
____ Overseas List $13.95 ____
____ Passport to Overseas Employment $14.95 ____
____ Work, Study, Travel Abroad $11.95 ____

MILITARY

____ Does Your Resume Wear Combat Boots? $7.95 ____
____ Re-Entry $13.95 ____
____ Retiring From the Military $22.95 ____
____ Woman's Guide to Military Service $10.95 ____
____ Young Person's Guide to the Military $9.95 ____

WOMEN AND SPOUSES

____ Back to Work $8.95 ____
____ Best Companies for Women $9.95 ____
____ Careers for Women Without College $10.95 ____
____ Female Advantage $19.95 ____
____ Getting Up When You're Feeling Down $17.95 ____
____ Relocating Spouse's Guide to Employment $12.95 ____
____ Women Changing Work $12.95 ____

COLLEGE STUDENTS

_____	College Majors and Careers	$16.95 _____
_____	How You Really Get Hired	$8.95 _____
_____	Internships	$27.95 _____
_____	Liberal Arts Jobs	$11.95 _____
_____	Put Your Degree to Work	$9.95 _____

JOB LISTINGS AND NEWSLETTERS

_____	Career Planning & Adult Development Newsletters (6 issues)	$30.00 _____
_____	Career Opportunities News (6 issues)	$30.00 _____
_____	Federal Career Opportunities (6 issues)	$37.00 _____
_____	Federal Jobs Digest (6 issues)	$29.00 _____
_____	International Employment Hotline (12 issues)	$29.00 _____

CHILDREN, YOUTH, AND SUMMER JOBS

_____	It's Your Future	$11.95 _____
_____	A Real Job for You	$9.95 _____
_____	Teenager's Guide to the Best Summer Opportunities	$9.95 _____

MINORITIES, IMMIGRANTS, DISABLED

_____	Black Woman's Career Guide	$14.95 _____
_____	Directory of Special Programs for Minority Group Members	$34.95 _____
_____	Finding A Job in the U.S.	$7.95 _____
_____	Job Hunting For the Disabled	$10.95 _____

EXPERIENCED AND ELDERLY

_____	40+ Job Hunting Guide	$21.95 _____
_____	Getting a Job After 50	$29.95 _____

ALTERNATIVE CAREER FIELDS AND ENTREPRENEURSHIP

_____	Avoiding the Pitfalls of Starting Your Own Business	$19.95 _____
_____	*"Career Choices for the 90s"* Series (all 12 titles)	$99.95 _____
_____	• Art	$8.95 _____
_____	• Business	$8.95 _____
_____	• Communications/Journalism	$8.95 _____
_____	• Computer Science	$8.95 _____
_____	• Economics	$8.95 _____
_____	• English	$8.95 _____
_____	• History	$8.95 _____
_____	• Law	$8.95 _____
_____	• Mathematics	$8.95 _____
_____	• MBA	$8.95 _____

_____	• Political Science/Government	$8.95 _____
_____	• Psychology	$8.95 _____
_____	**Career Directory Series** (all 8 titles)	$157.95 _____
_____	• Advertising	$19.95 _____
_____	• Book Publishing	$19.95 _____
_____	• Business & Finance	$19.95 _____
_____	• Magazine Publishing	$19.95 _____
_____	• Marketing	$19.95 _____
_____	• Newspaper Publishing	$19.95 _____
_____	• Public Relations	$19.95 _____
_____	• Travel & Hospitality	$19.95 _____
_____	**"Career Opportunities in..."** **Series** (all 4 titles)	$137.95 _____
_____	• Art	$27.95 _____
_____	• Music Industry	$27.95 _____
_____	• TV, Cable, and Video	$27.95 _____
_____	• Writing	$27.95 _____
_____	**"Careers In..."** **Series** (all 8 titles)	$132.95 _____
_____	• Careers in Accounting	$16.95 _____
_____	• Careers in Business	$16.95 _____
_____	• Careers in Communications	$16.95 _____
_____	• Careers in Computers	$16.95 _____
_____	• Careers in Education	$16.95 _____
_____	• Careers in Engineering	$16.95 _____
_____	• Careers in Health Care	$16.95 _____
_____	• Careers in Science	$16.95 _____
_____	Careers With Robots	$26.95 _____
_____	Flying High in Travel	$14.95 _____
_____	How to Become a Successful Consultant	$19.95 _____
_____	Job Opportunities for Business & Liberal Arts Graduates	$19.95 _____
_____	Job Opportunities for Engineering, Science, and Computer Graduates	$19.95 _____
_____	Making It in the Media Professions	$18.95 _____
_____	New Accountant Careers	$13.95 _____
_____	**"Opportunities in..."** **Series** (136+ titles: $12.95 each or $1749.95 for set; contact publisher)	$1749.95 _____
_____	Outdoor Career Guide	$20.95 _____
_____	Planning Your Medical Career	$17.95 _____

SUBTOTAL _____

Virginia residents add
4½% sales tax _____

POSTAGE/HANDLING ($3.00 for
first title and $.50 for each $3.00
additional book) _____

TOTAL ENCLOSED _____